WALK
YOURSELF
THIN

WALK
YOURSELF
THIN

David A. Rives

Moon River Publishing
Ventura, California

Distributed by
PRICE STERN SLOAN
Los Angeles

Printed in the United States of America
10 9 8 7 6 5 4 3 2 1

ISBN 0-8431-3360-0

"This above all: To thine own self be true."
Hamlet

Dedication

I'd like to thank my wife, Catherine, and my sons, Adam and Graham, for giving me the "space" to finish this book; and my mother, Stella, who always wanted to.

But I'd especially like to dedicate the book to:

1) My sister, Karen, whose lifelong weight problem has been as much a challenge to me as my own.

2) The late Louis Goldberg of Detroit, who, in one 5-minute conversation some 30 years ago, showed me more of life's possibilities than anyone ever has, before or since — proving once again that when the advice is right, you don't need years of it!

Thank you, Lou; sorry you couldn't stick around to see what you unwittingly wrought.

And thank you, S. L., for taking that little bit of extra time to get ready for our one and only date.

Table of Contents

Chap.	Title	Page
1	"All Aboard!"	1
2	Before You Start	3
3	"Vive la Difference!"	5
4	"What's it to You?!"	7
5	"Let's Take a Walk"	9
6	Thinwalking	12
7	"Go Tell it to Your Body!"	15
8	"Details! Details!"	18
9	For the "Progressoholic"	20
10	What to Expect	23
11	"Say 'Cheese!'"	26
12	"A Year to Go"	28
13	"Murphy's Law"	30
14	A Word about Weighing	33
15	Further Thoughts on Weighing	34
16	The Dawn of a "New Age"	39
17	Why Thinwalking Works	42
18	The Fly in the Ointment	45
19	Why Diets Don't Work	48
20	"...from the Black Lagoon!"	54
21	Wrapping it Up	57
22	The Magic of Thinwalking	59
23	"Can we Talk?"	63
24	"Watch Out!"	65

Chap.	Title	Page
25	Goals	67
26	Control	68
27	The Best Thing	70
28	"...and Twice on Sundays!"	72
29	"To Your Health!"	74
30	Other Exercises	76
31	A Way Out	78
32	"Christmas"	79
33	For the Few	81
34	Going on a "Diet"	85
35	"If You Can...."	89
36	"Breakfast"	98
37	"No Sweat!"	100
38	"Why, Indeed?!"	103
39	If You Smoke	106
40	"It's a Boy!"	108
41	That Time of Month	110
42	The Kiddie Korps	112
43	When You're Thin	115
44	One Last Word	117
45	About the Log	119
46	The Daily Log	121-134
	Appendix A	135
	Index	137
	Glossary	149

1
All Aboard!

You're about to set off on a remarkable journey; a "walking tour" of a wonderful new world, where you will:

* Get thin forever, without changing a thing about the way you eat!
* Take the part of your mind that makes you eat and turn it into your **best friend**, instead of your **worst enemy**, the way all "diets" do!
* Feel **better** and **better** as the inches disappear, not **worse** and **worse**!
* Finally enjoy all the wonderful things thin people enjoy, **just because they're thin**!

With the Walk Yourself Thin program, the last reason for staying fat — "I can't stop eating" — has become meaningless, since you can keep eating whatever you want to eat and still get as thin as you want to get.

Just Thinwalk for one enjoyable hour a day and you'll give yourself a body you can be proud of, a body you'll want to look at, put clothes on, take out in public, share with others.

The streets and running tracks of America are filling up with Thinwalkers (people walking themselves thin) — all knowing the joy of eating exactly what they want, with none suffering the obesity that used to go with it.

We invite you to join us on those streets, that track, to begin a life you've only dreamed of, a life where you can finally "have your cake and eat it too!"

2

"Before you Start"

You're about to Walk Yourself Thin. Which means you're going to have to change your lifestyle a teensy, tiny bit — take a more active role in shaping your future.

Because of that, and because the lawyers inform me that this world has gotten kind of sue-happy lately, there's one thing I've got to tell you:

Like any program where you have to move a tad faster than a glacier, you could be looking at a possible health risk.

So before you do anything, you really should tell your family doctor what you're about to do — get his "seal of approval."

And now that we've covered our rears with the standard "see-your-doctor" number, you want to know what we **really** think about it?!

We hate it!

Why?

Oh, not because it isn't necessary; it is!

But if you're like most of us "chunkers," you're already looking for any reason under the Sun **not** to get thin, and "see your doctor first" is **all** you've got to hear:

"You know, I'd love to get thin, Marge, but I have to see my doctor first and he doesn't have an opening till just after the turn of the century! So there you have it, pass me a cookie!"

While we don't want you killing yourself, we'd like you to keep one thing in mind: Thinwalking is such a mild exercise that very few of you will wind up on the wrong side of an oxygen tent because of it!

In fact, those "rolls" you keep adding to are far more likely to get you "tented" than all the walking you could ever do!

So the next time it comes down to a choice between "cookies" and "walking," you might want to see what "walking" can do for you — "doctor" or no "doctor" — since there aren't any surprises left in the cookie jar!

It's funny: someone like Sara Lee never has to tell you to "see your doctor" before you eat any of **her** stuff.   And yet, her stuff makes people fat, and fat people seem to die a whole lot sooner than thin people, if I read those charts right, and yet she gets **awards** for her stuff, while "exercise pushers" have to tiptoe past courtrooms!

I guess old Sara figures we're all smart enough to know that we should "take" her products in teensy, tiny "doses," and if we abuse them, that's our problem, not hers. Which, of course, is the same way liquor companies think, and tobacco companies, and wine companies, and beer companies and anyone else selling something that's incredibly addictive.

And, since they all seem to get away with it, I guess they're right: it **is** our fault! Shame on us!

Now me, all I'm "selling" is "health." So I've got to warn you that if you do what the Creator gave you a body to do — move around — so you can get that body looking the way the Creator most likely wants it to look — slim — you might be the one-in-a-million who shouldn't have. And the only way we're going to know that is if you let your doctor check you out.

So do it.

But while you're waiting for him to check **you** out, you might want to check **us** out; you know: put one foot in front of the other for a minute or two!

Then, if "Doc" says you're **not** that one-in-a-million, you'll be that many miles closer to a Beautiful New You!

3
"Vive la Difference!"

Before you start, we've got to tell you: you can forget about losing weight with Thinwalking!
"What?!"
That's right.
"Nice to see ya!"
No, don't leave! Hear us out!
"Wel-l-l-l....."
That's better.

All we're saying is that Thinwalking isn't a typical weight-loss program — what you would call a "diet." It's an **exercise** program and exercise programs work differently than "diets:"

Every day, your body has to burn a certain number of calories to keep you alive and kicking. Feed your body fewer calories than it'll be burning — which is what "diets" make you do — and the only place the body can go to for the "missing" calories is the fat it's been storing, every time you've overeaten.

Give your body a pound's-worth of calories when it needs to burn two, and, with any luck, your body will pull a pound of fat out of storage and burn that to make up the shortfall.

So what's different about Thinwalking?
Only everything:

Oh, not the part about fat-burning; that stays the same. It's the **reason** for the fat-burning that changes:

With the "diet," you burned fat to make up for some calories you didn't eat; with Thinwalking, you burn fat to build up leg muscles you've been exercising.

So what?

Well, with the "diet," you had only one thing happening: a pound of fat disappearing, which meant you lost a pound of weight.

With Thinwalking, two things happen: that pound of fat still disappears, but now a pound of new muscle shows up in its place!

"So?"

So at the end of each Thinwalking day, instead of being "one pound 'short,'" like you were on your "diet," you find that you're "**no** pounds 'short'" — but you're still one "pound" **skinnier!**

"Wait a minute: how can that be? How can I be skinnier without losing any weight?!"

Easy! Because

A pound of muscle takes up a lot less space than a pound of fat.

So every time you "trade" a pound of fat for a pound of muscle, like you do with Thinwalking, you lose a lot of **size** without losing any **weight!**

"Oh-h-h."

That's why we tell you to forget about losing weight with Thinwalking, because you probably **won't** lose any — especially when you first get started!

All you'll lose is body **size** — great, gobbing hunks of bodysize — and you'll lose it more easily, more permanently and more naturally than with all the "diets" ever invented!

This may be hard to take at first — losing size without losing weight — but as you grow more and more gorgeous, you'll learn to live with it!

Everyone else has!

4
"What's it to You?!"

By the way: Why do you care whether I'm fat or thin? I mean, what's it to you? Why can't you just leave me alone and let me live my own life?"

Good questions.
Here's a good answer:

Because I have to live in your world, and a world filled with fat people is a world filled with anger and meanness and spite and depression and failed opportunities, failed relationships, failed families, and...do I have to go on?
"No, we get the message. But you forgot one thing:"
What's that?"
"I'm happy being fat!"

Sure you are!
You're "happy" that it takes you "ten minutes" to get out of a chair;
You're "happy" that that pin on the floor might just as well be on the Moon, for all the chance you've got of bending down and picking it up;
You're "happy" that you have to huff and puff your way through 40 job interviews before you finally get hired on as a file clerk; I mean, all you've got going for you is an MBA from Harvard!;

You're "happy" that people always seem to need a fill-up on their coffee the minute you get near them;

You're "happy" that you have to sit for hours, making your own clothes, because nobody ever dreamed that people your size would actually care what they wore!

Sure you're "happy!"

"Adjusted," maybe. But "adjusted" isn't "happy!:"

"Adjusted" is convincing yourself that **everybody** has a hard time, getting into and out of these "new little cars;"

"Adjusted" is telling yourself that, "If there's something wrong with making twenty trips to the salad bar, why doesn't the manager stop me?;"

"Adjusted" is becoming funnier than everybody else, so at least **one** person has a full cup when you enter the room!

"So I'm 'happy' that I'm 'adjusted!' What's wrong with that?"

Nothing. Except that you'd be happier if you were **happy**!

"And how do I do that?"

By getting thin, for starters.

No, let's be honest about that: getting thin won't automatically make you happy! All getting thin will do is take away the **un**happiness of being fat. But you'd be amazed at how much happiness can enter your life when it doesn't have to climb over mountains of misery to get there!

And how do you get rid of at least one of those "mountains?"

Easy: By walking yourself thin!

And, while you're walking, you might want to burn something on your brain: It's our own variation of a fairly popular bumper sticker ("The worst day fishing is better than the best day working!")

Ours reads:

"The worst day thin is better than the best day fat!"

As you walk yourself thin, you'll know exactly what we're talking about!

5

"Let's Take a Walk"

You've got to face one thing: If you're going to get thin, you're going to have to **control** something: either your "gonzo" eating or your less-than-"gonzo" exercising!

Since you obviously don't want to control **anything**, we'd be kind of stupid to pick the one that's the **hardest** to control!

"Which is?"

Well, how do you feel about giving up your omelets and muffins and cookies and candy and rolls and butter and french fries and pizza and—

"STOP IT!"

That's what we thought! Next question: Would you have any problem, taking a nice, refreshing walk every day?

"None that I can think of."

Fine. And, since that "nice, refreshing walk" will get you just as thin as giving up all the food in Fargo, why torture yourself!?

"Hey: You've got **my** vote! When do we start?"

Very soon.

"One question, though:"

Yes?

"Why 'walking?' Why not 'jogging?' Or 'swimming?' Or 'skiing?' Or 'biking?' Or 'rowing?' I mean, all you're talking about is 'exercising yourself thin,' right?"

Right.

"So what difference does it make **which** exercise you choose?"

Makes no difference at all — as long as you choose the **best** one.

"Which is...?"

Well, why are we talking exercise in the first place?

"So we can burn calories to get thin."

Very good. So what would an exercise have to do to be the "best" exercise?

"I guess, be the one that burns the **most** calories."

That's right. And not just "per session," but "per year/decade/etc."

And what would keep "biking" or "swimming" or "jogging" or "skiing" or "rowing" from being the "best" exercise?

Well, how much time do you think joggers spend, nursing injuries?;

See a lot of skiers when there's no snow, do you?;

Oh, it was "**water** skiing" you were referring to? Terrific exercise! All you need is a boat and a driver and a line and skis and a body of water and a nice day and...;

"Swimming?" There's that "body of water" again!;

"Biking?" No problem: as long as you have a bike and it's working;

"Rowing?" Another "winner!" Care to guess how many rowing machines are still being used, a month after they're brought home?

You get the picture: an exercise isn't much good if you're not doing it. And if there's a million reasons **not** to do something, the chances are awfully good you won't! Which means you won't be burning any calories and won't be getting thin.

And what's to stop you from walking? Well, aside from the obvious — blizzards, hurricanes and the like — nothing comes to mind! All you have to do is strap on a decent pair of shoes, dress appropriately and step out your front door!

So, at the end of a year's time, who do you think will have burned more calories: the running/skiing/swimming/rowing /

biking "hare" — who spends more time on the "shelf" than on the "mark" — or the Thinwalking "tortoise," who just takes a nice brisk walk every day — day after day after day after day after day...............?

That's right!

So who's done the "best" exercise?

You got it!

So forget about how good an exercise looks on paper ("Burn Seven Million Calories an Hour, Cross-country Skiing!"); the paper's **already** thin!

Just go out and Thinwalk every day and you'll burn more calories than all the skiers, bikers, joggers, swimmers and rowers **combined**!

Of course, as you walk yourself thin, you'll start to feel so good about yourself, so "energized," that you'll be "chafing at the bit" to do some of those other exercises.

So — DO THEM! Do every one of them you think you might enjoy!

Just one thing, though:

Don't do any of them to **get** thin; do them only after you **are** thin! That way, you won't jeopardize your Get-thin Program halfway through by switching from an exercise you can and will do every day — Thinwalking — to an exercise you can't or won't!

Other than that: Exercise away! That's what getting thin is all about!

6
"Thinwalking"

Oh sure: 'walking!' Know all about it! Been doing it all my life!"

Fine. But if you're not thin, we'll bet you haven't been walking fast enough or far enough for your walking to be classed as "exercise."

And how fast and how far would that be?

Well, to turn "walking" into "Thinwalking," all you have to do is

WALK AS FAST AS YOU COMFORTABLY CAN FOR AS LONG AS YOU COMFORTABLY CAN!

"That's it?!"

That's it.

"Doesn't sound like much."

Oh, but it is:

1) When you walk as fast as you **comfortably** can (and that speed will change every minute you're walking), you'll always be burning the **most fat calories you can**; go any slower and you won't be burning the "max;" go any faster and you'll start to burn **non**-fat calories (muscle tissue), which is the **last** thing you want to do!

2) By walking only as **long** as you comfortably can, you'll burn up the most fat calories you can **at each session** without jeopar-

dizing your **next** session by "overdoing" it.

Since you never **lose** any sessions, you wind up burning the most fat calories you can per year, millenium, etc., which is the way you get thin and stay thin.

A word of advice, though:

No matter how fast you'll be going at the peak of your walk, start out slowly and work up to that speed gradually. That way, your muscles won't "burn out" sooner than they should have, leaving calories on your body and not on the road or track where they belong!

When you begin your Thinwalking program, your legs will feel sore at the start of each session. Don't worry: this soreness will work its way out as you walk, so don't ever let it keep you on the couch.

(In fact, a lot of people tell me they wind up having their **best** Thinwalking sessions on days they've felt their **worst** going in ["tired," "listless," "ache-y," etc.]! I don't know why this is so; it just is.

(And because it is, you should always think twice before passing up a Thinwalk because you "don't feel like it!" You could be cheating yourself out of a fun workout, and, more important, keeping Thinwalking from doing its job of knocking hundreds of calories off you!)

After about a month, soreness will stop being a problem, and you can just concentrate on walking faster and farther.

And speaking of "faster" and "farther:" take your time going for world-class mileages and speeds. A little ways into the program, you'll be walking distances and speeds that will **astound** you, so don't worry if you can't do them on Day One or Week One. They will come; just let your **body** tell you when, not the other way around.

Remember: you're here for one thing and one thing only: to get thin.

As long as you walk as fast as you comfortably can for as long as you comfortably can every day, that's exactly what you'll do!

And when you do, you'll know how those athletes feel who stand on three-tiered platforms every four years — freshly-minted medals dangling from their necks — and tearfully watch their country's flags being raised, their anthems played.

Because that's exactly the way getting thin will make you feel — especially if no one thought you could!

7

"Go Tell it to your Body"

One of the great miracles of life is that your body does exactly what you "tell" it to do.

When you Thinwalk, you're "telling" your body: "I'm going to be **using** these legs, so you better do whatever you can to **help** me use them!"

And your body does!

How?

By giving you the tools to walk farther and faster each time you go out:

Walking takes energy.

Your muscles get this energy from "power molecules" that they store.

As you Thinwalk, these molecules — which we call "glycogen" or animal starch — get used up.

When they're **all** used up, you've walked "as long as you comfortably can" and you might as well stop (distance runners call this "Hitting the 'Wall;'" you'll know why, when it happens to you!)

So there you stand, with "empty" leg muscles.

And what does your body do when it "sees" that?

It starts replacing the glycogen.

But does it put back exactly what your walk took out?

No! It puts back **more** than you took out.

15

Why?

Because it **always assumes** you'll be walking even **farther** your next time out, and those **extra miles** will need **extra fuel!**

And that's not the only assumption the body makes:

Whenever you "challenge" your muscles, there will always be a certain number of them that are not up to the challenge; these will break down.

When your body "sees" these broken muscles, it will sweep them away and build new ones in their place.

But will your body build new muscles that are the same size and strength as the old ones?

Not at all! It will build **bigger** and **stronger** muscles — and more of them!

Why?

Because it **always assumes** you'll need to walk even **faster** your next time out, and it has to provide the **extra strength** to go that **extra speed!**

Because of this "double 'overkill'" — putting back more glycogen than you took out and building stronger muscles than you broke down — you find yourself with muscles that couldn't "drag" you five **feet** on Day One, suddenly "whizzing" you five **miles** on Day **Twenty**-one!

And all because you "told" your body that that's where you were headed!

The next question, of course, is:

Where does all this new glycogen come from, and where do you get the energy and raw materials to do all the muscle rebuilding?

The answer: from your fat pads:

1) After your walk, the body pulls some fat out of storage, changes it to glycogen and ships it off to its new home in the muscle, where it can fuel the rebuilding and your next walk.

2) The body pulls more fat out of storage, changes it into protein and uses that to make new muscles.

And there you have it — the whole Thinwalking Story in a nutshell:

"Exercised muscles pulling fat from storage in order to 're-charge their batteries' and build themselves up!"

And how does that get you thin? Very easily:
Since exercised muscles are thinner than the fat they "pull,"

The more you exercise, the thinner you get!

—until you eventually use up **all** your visible fat (the body always keeps a little bit "hidden away" for emergencies) and wind up with the sleekest, most gorgeous legs and body your "biology" will allow!

And all because of one simple thing: the fact that you got out there and "talked" to your body every day — one Thinwalking step after another!

8

"Details! Details!"

What is "Thinwalking?"

"Walking as fast as you comfortably can for as long as you comfortably can."

Good. And because of that, there are two things you should watch out for:

First: because you're only going "as fast as you **comfortably** can," you never need to time yourself: if your pace gets **too** comfortable, you speed up; if it gets **un**comfortable, you slow down. It doesn't really matter how fast you're going, because you're not trying to break any speed records.

Second: because you're only walking "as **far** as you comfortably can," you don't need to keep track of mileage: you walk as far as you comfortably can and not a step further. Whatever the mileage is, it is, and **knowing** what it is won't add a single inch to the total!

The other way of going about it — worrying about "times" and "mileage" — can drive you crazy, because all of a sudden you've got daily targets to hit or you won't feel like you're making any progress.

And what happens if you don't hit those targets?

Well, what always happens when you fall short of a goal? That's right: you get discouraged and depressed and go off on an eating binge!

To make sure that doesn't happen, we ask that you forget about all **other** targets for once and just concentrate on **Thinwalking's** target: getting you thin!

And how do you hit **that** target? By doing nothing more than going out every day and walking as fast as you comfortably can for as long as you comfortably can. In other words, by letting your **body** tell you how well you're doing each day — not yesterday's performance charts!

And what will your body tell you each day?
That you're always doing **the best you can**, given the conditions of **that day** (weather; mental attitude; physical shape). And how much better can you do than "**the best you can**?!"

So don't be obsessed by "times" and "mileage."
Just Thinwalk every day and pretty soon you'll find out what every other Thinwalker has found out: that Thinwalking is a **joy**, and as long as you don't do anything that takes the joy **out** of Thinwalking — like worrying about "progress" — you'll want to do it forever! And stay thin forever!

If you can think of a **better** way to spend the rest of your life, you've got our address!

9
"For the 'Progressoholic'"

Now where ya going?

"To buy one of those nifty 'sports' watches that lets me keep track of ' lap times' and 'mileage!'"

But I just told you—

"Yeah, right! Hey: do me a favor?—"

What?

"—Work me up some kind of 'program' for when I get back with the watch."

Oh. Sure.

Well, nobody else seems to listen when you tell them that curiosity killed the cat, so why should you?!

Just promise us one thing: You want to keep track of your progress? Go ahead. But we weren't kidding:

Your "progress" should be measured in "clothing sizes," not "lap times" or "total mileage." And, if becoming a "slave" to one keeps you from achieving the other, then you should take your "nifty 'sports' watch" and throw it into a nifty **river**!

Now that we've gotten that out of our system...

To measure your progress from day to day, you have to walk a set circuit — what we call a "loop." This can be around your own neighborhood or a nearby park or a school running track.

It doesn't matter how long this loop is, only that it's a fixed distance, so that you can compare your performance on it from one day to the next (you should have a few of these loops, for variety.)

(If you do want to know how far you're walking each day, drive your loop in a car and record its mileage. Then multiply that by the number of times you walk it.

(If the loop is not driveable [in a park, for example], then reverse the process: figure out how long it takes you to walk a mile at your normal walking speed [a school's quarter-mile track is best for this,] then time how long it takes you to walk around your undriveable loop at about that same speed.

(When you've got the time for that unknown loop, just divide it by your normal mile time and you'll get a rough idea how long your new loop is.

(We'll make it simple: if you know it takes you 16 minutes to walk a mile and you can get around your new loop in 12 minutes, then your new loop is about "12/16ths" — or "3/4" — of a mile).

The next step is to figure out how to use the sports watch (none of them is difficult to use; just work along with the instructions) and to start recording your "lap times," "total laps," "total time," "total mileage" (we've included a Walking Log with this book, to help you keep track of these.)

Just don't forget: your performance will vary from day to day, depending on a lot of things (weather; lung capacity; leg condition; companions; etc.,) so don't expect your progress chart to look like a 747 taking off (a child's version of the Rocky Mountains would be more like it!)

We'll say it again: Your best bet is to just go out every day and walk as fast as you comfortably can for as long as you comfortably can.

If you want to record your "lap times," etc., go ahead and record them; just don't be **obsessed** by them and don't expect that every day will be better than the one before it.

And, if you find that your "bad" days **are** making you discouraged, you know the way to the river!

The purpose of Thinwalking is to get you thin and keep you thin — not to make you upset that you won't be in the next Olympics (though as we've told you: once you're a little ways into the program, you'll start chalking up speeds and distances that are impressive by anyone's standards. The only thing is: you may be walking those speeds and distances only every other day, or every third day, and unless you realize that and can accept it, you'll find yourself getting forever "disappointed.")

So if you "can't live" without charting your progress, then do it. But if you find yourself cancelling Thinwalking sessions because you're afraid you won't be able to "perform" on a given day, then **stop** playing with your charts and get back to doing what Thinwalking is designed to do: get you **thin**!

Which is exactly what will happen if you just walk as fast as you comfortably can for as long as you comfortably can each day — no matter how "fast" or "long" that might be!

10
What to Expect

What should you expect from Thinwalking?

Well, we can tell you what **not** to expect. Mainly:

Don't expect to get thin overnight.

We know that's the way you'd like it to happen (who wouldn't?), but it's not going to, so don't expect it.

In fact, "real-world" slimming — Thinwalking slimming — happens so gradually (in "ounces per day"), that you're better off if you

Don't expect to see ANY change in body size, EVER!

Why?

Because nobody yet born can tell when the Pacific Ocean is "down a quart!"

It's a little like the experiment where you blindfold someone and prick the skin over his thumb with a pin; then you move the pin a real small amount and ask him if it moved.

If you do it just right, he'll say "No," because our senses aren't fine enough to pick up on such small changes.

You keep going, moving the pin a little bit each time, and each time he says, "No, the pin didn't move."

When you're done, you tell him to take off the blindfold. And what he sees is the pin — that started at his **thumb** and that he said "never moved" — now sitting on his **shoulder**!

That's the way Thinwalking works: you start out fat and wind up thin and you never knew what hit you! So don't **expect** to! Because if you do, you'll find yourself getting disappointed.

So what?

Well what always happens when you get disappointed?

That's right: you quit!

And try as we might, we've never been able to figure out a way for Thinwalking to get you thin if you're not doing it!

So do us a favor: Walk for any reason you can think of —

Walk because your heart and lungs will love you for it;

Walk because your legs will get "'goose-y' gorgeous;"

Walk because it eases your mind;

Walk because it "helps your hormones;"

Walk so that your kids will want to;

Walk because your life is better **with** a walking program than it is **without** one;

—walk for any reason you want to, except one: to get thin.

Why?

Because if you walk for that reason, you'll always be disappointed and will always give up. But if you don't, you won't, since all those other goals are easy to achieve.

And what will happen while you're achieving those **other** goals? Of course: you'll "secretly" achieve the one you **really** want: getting thin forever!

We hate to make it look like you have to "sneak up" on thinness, but that's the way it works: Expect Thinwalking to get you thin and it probably won't; expect it to do anything else and people will be admiring the New You from morning to night!

And what's the best way to get Thinwalking doing what you want it to do?

Easy: Just make it a normal part of your daily routine, along with all the other activities you don't have any "special expectations" for; things like brushing your teeth, taking a shower, shopping, eating, etc.

If you can do that — if you can make Thinwalking a normal part of your everyday life — then it will do everything you want it to do, including getting you slim and trim.

But if you can't — if you insist on making Thinwalking something it's not — the chances are real good that it won't do a thing!

And do you really need another one of **those** in your life?!

11
"Say Cheese!"

Of course, if you really want to see what Thinwalking is doing for you, there is a way:

Take pictures of yourself!

Specifically: have someone take your picture once a month from a variety of different angles: face-on; three-quarter front; side; three-quarter rear; rear. Wear as few clothes as modesty (and the photo developer) will allow, since we want to see changes in your body, not your wardrobe!

Take some of the photos with your arms at your sides, some with your arms in the air. Take some bust shots, some from the waist up, some full-body. Strike some poses, like the models do in magazines.

In this way, and only in this way, will you be able to see the progress everyone else has been seeing since the day you started Thinwalking.

One more thing about taking pictures: because slimming is so gradual with Thinwalking, not only won't you believe anything is happening while it's happening, you won't believe anything has happened once it's **done**!

That's why it's especially important to take pictures of yourself after you get down to normal body size, because that's the only way you'll know how far you've come (you can't do it by looking at yourself in the mirror because you can't see all of yourself at one time, like you can with a snapshot).

Unless you're made of stone, it won't take long for you to **fall in love** with what you see in those photos!

That's OK; don't be embarrassed!

The whole point of this program is to get you to love others, so they can love you, and no one in the history of the world has ever been able to truly love someone else without loving himself first!

So do it! Let yourself go! Cry for joy, if you feel like it!

You've "reclaimed" yourself! Celebrate it!

And then take somebody **else's** picture!

12

"A Year to Go"

Quick review:

What's the only way that Thinwalking can fail?

"If you expect more from it than it can possibly deliver."

Very good! And what is the best way to stop that from happening?

"Get a lobotomy?"

Well, yes. But before that.

"Don't have a clue."

The best way we've found, to remove all fatal expectations from Thinwalking, is to tell yourself that, no matter what body size you are, you

Always have a year to go

to get down to your **ideal** body size:

If you're a hundred size-pounds overweight (see Appendix A), you have "a year to go" to get them off;

If you lose half those hundred, you still have "a year to go" to get rid of the other 50;

When you are only 10 size-pounds over your ideal body size, you have "a year to go" to take those off!;

And when you have only **one** size-pound left to lose, you still have "**a year to go**" to get rid of it!!

Always having "a year to go" takes all the weight-loss "pressure" off you, and lets you enjoy what Thinwalking is **really** doing for you: beautifying your leg muscles and strengthening your heart muscle (which will soon stop trying to pound its way out of your chest, every time you so much as roll over in bed!)

Of course, in order to achieve its **primary** goals, Thinwalking has to do one small thing: empty out all your fat stores. Which gives you a nifty little **side effect**, known as: "Thinness!"

And to make sure you do get that "side effect," just keep telling yourself, every time you look in the mirror and and see a body that's larger than it should be:

"No problem: I still have a year to go to get thin!"

Until, one day, you are!

13
"Murphy's Law"

Your body pulls fat from its various storehouses in a built-in sequence. For one person, that sequence might be: "head-chest-neck-calves-etc.;" for another, it could be just the reverse.

However, no matter what your individual fat-pulling sequence is, we all seem to be victims of a "Murphy's Law" ("If anything can go wrong, it will.")

In the case of bodysize loss, our "Murphy's Law" reads:

"Wherever you really want the bodysize to leave, that's where it won't!"

All you have to do, for example, if you want your thighs to stay as fat as Nature can make them, is to wish with all your heart that they would get thin!

Day after Thinwalking day you'll stare at those thighs and day after day the verdict will be the same: "No change!"

Everywhere else? "No problem!:" your arms, shoulders, neck, chest will get as slim as it's possible to get, and do it in record time!

But those thighs? Forget it!

And Heaven help you if you want the bodysize to come off your **waistline**! We wish we had a dollar for everyone who lost 4-6 inches from his chest, 3-4 inches from each thigh, but **not one millimeter** from his waistline while everything else was "evaporating!"

In fact, if you're expecting to see any change at all in your waistline, expect it to look **bigger** before it looks smaller. Why? Because, as Einstein said: "Everything is relative:"

When you look at your waistline in a mirror, you judge how big it is by comparing it with structures around it, like your chest.

If your lower chest has gotten four inches smaller since you started Thinwalking, but your waistline only one, then your waistline will actually look like it's gotten three inches **bigger** since the day you began!

Which will, of course, do wonders for your spirits!:

"What the hell's going on here?! I'm walking like there's no tomorrow, and all I'm getting is **fatter**?! Let me off this stupid 'bus!'"

And you'll start making plans for that hour you used to waste every day, trying to walk yourself thin.

And while you're making those plans, you'll slip on a pair of slacks that were tight just last week, and you'll get ready for a real "fight" when you go to button them, since you're obviously fatter than you were the last time you wore them.

Except that when you do go to button them you **don't** have to "fight;" in fact, the two sides come together rather easily.

And you'll look at those slacks in the mirror and, when you've convinced yourself that they're the same ones you had on the week before, and that no one's stretched them while you were out, your eyes will travel up from those slacks to look stunned at themselves:

"Ohmigod: it **does** work!"

And you'll get a cold feeling up and down your spine.

"What if I **had** 'gotten off' the 'bus?' How much bodysize would I have **kept** myself from losing?!"

Answer: "All of it!"

So don't ever leave the program because of what you **think** is happening! Remember: "seeing" isn't always "believing," especially in the case of your waistline, where you're forever seeing it next to other "structures," not next to what **it** looked like two weeks ago (that's why **pictures** are so important).

The fact is: **all** the bodysize will go eventually and no one will care what order it went in (or how "lumpy" you looked in the meantime!)

The way it will happen is that, once all the **non**-"Murphy" storehouses have been emptied of their fat, the body will finally turn its attention to the places **you've** been wanting it to leave for so long.

Suddenly, areas that couldn't lose "millimeters-per-month" (thighs; waistline; etc.) will be dropping "inches-per-week," and you won't be able to update your wardrobe fast enough (do we have to tell you what a glorious day **that** is?!)

And if you didn't get a shudder before, you'll sure get one now:

"My God: What if I **had** given up because it 'wasn't working?' This day would never have come!!"

That's right!

So don't risk that "day" by ignoring "Murphy's Law of Bodysize Loss" or "Einstein's Corollary."

Just keep Thinwalking every day and you'll soon be able to tell Murphy exactly where **he** can "get off!"

14
A Word about Weighing Yourself

DON'T

15
Further Thoughts
On Weighing Yourself

hough the last chapter was as complete as it needed to be (feel free to review it any time you want), we'd like to take a moment to expand on a few of its key points:

There are several reasons why you should never weigh yourself, on this or any other program:

1. There is nothing more meaningless than body **weight**; the only important thing is body **size**.

To show you what we mean:
Take your typical football halfback and the "couch potato" who watches him perform every autumn Sunday:
A likely height and weight for each of them would be 5'11" and 210 pounds.
If weight really meant anything, then both men would wear the same size clothes, get the same looks from the ladies, move with the same style and grace, etc.
And do they? Yeah, right!:
The halfback slips easily into Size 32 slacks, while the couch potato can only dream about getting into his Size 38's; women line up at the halfback's door, while the couch potato can't get a nod from his goldfish; the halfback moves like a racehorse, while the couch potato sits and waits for a plow!

Why the difference?

Well, obviously: the halfback is 210 pounds of "muscle," the couch potato 210 pounds of "fat."

What does this tell you? Simply that, **on a pound-for-pound basis**, "muscle" takes up a lot less space than "fat."

So if our couch potato could just "trade" every pound of billowy fat for a pound of lean, hard muscle, he could get a whole lot thinner without getting any lighter!

And can he make that "trade?" Sure he can: with Thinwalking. And so can you.

Since all you'll be doing, with Thinwalking, is "trading" pounds of bulging fat for pounds of lean muscle, what sense would it make to weigh yourself? Your **weight** will never change; only your **body size** will.

So don't do it, especially since weighing yourself can be such a "killer" (read on!)

2. The second reason for never weighing yourself is:

You don't know what you're weighing!

If you were weighing just "body fat" every time you stepped on a scale, and your weight went up or stayed the same after some serious dieting or exercise, then you could say for sure that that "diet" or that exercise program didn't work.

But **are** you weighing just body fat? Or are you weighing everything **else** under the sun: bones, muscles, organs, body fluids, gut contents?

Of course!

So when you step on a scale after dieting or exercise and the results are the opposite of what you were expecting, can you really say for sure that your weight-loss program didn't work (didn't eliminate fat)?

Or could your weight gain be due to some extra fluid your body has held back, to "process" a load of salt (it takes **ten** water molecules to process **one** molecule of salt, you know)? What about food going in but not coming out (delayed bowel movement); you think three pounds of food isn't going to weigh three pounds, just because it's now inside you?!

The bottom line is: changes in weight can be due to a lot of things — not just "fat loss" — and unless you realize that, you will be facing "terminal disappointment" when those changes don't go your way.

And what happens when someone or something disappoints you? Of course: you "console" yourself with about a hundred pounds of "garbage!"

Later on, when you pass the fluid or food that was giving you the false readings and discover that you really **did** lose weight (body fat) on your "diet" or exercise program, it'll be too late: the "hundred pounds of garbage" will again rule the roost, and you'll be back to where you've **always** been: pouring in the calories, but with no "diet" or exercise program to get rid of them!

To keep that from happening — to keep from giving up a reducing program because you thought it wasn't working or was working "in reverse" — trust the fact that when you weigh yourself you have no idea what you're weighing and never do it, since doing it can be disastrous!

3. Of the three things that weighing yourself can tell you — that you've lost weight, stayed the same, or gained weight — all can destroy your get-thin program.

We just saw how destructive it could be if you expected to lose weight and either stayed the same or gained weight.

But what happens if you diet or exercise like crazy and actually **lose** weight!? How could that be a "killer?!"

Very easily:

Actually doing what you set out to do — in this case, "losing weight" — is always cause for celebration, isn't it? And how do you

celebrate **everything?** Of course: with an extra-special **food** treat!
And why shouldn't you, since your lovely weight loss has actually
given you room to "cheat" a little!

Of course, when your mind and body get a taste of that
"forbidden fruit" once again, what are they going to do: not ask for
more?! Don't be silly! Give them one little hot fudge sundae and
they'll clamor for another one and another one, until that's **all** you're
eating!

Nothing wrong with that, except the Walk Yourself Thin
program promises that you'll get thin only if you **don't change your
eating habits!** In other words, if you had ten hot fudge sundaes last
year, you can have ten hot fudge sundaes this year. But not "ten hot
fudge sundaes a **week**," because **nothing** could overcome that!

To keep that from happening — to avoid a "celebration"
getting out of hand and destroying your get-thin program — never
give yourself a **reason** to "celebrate."

In other words: **stay away from the scale!**

At one time, we weren't so insistent about never weighing
yourself. Then we learned of a woman who dropped four dress sizes
by Thinwalking, got on a scale, discovered that she hadn't lost any
"weight" and immediately abandoned her walking program because
it "didn't work!"

Are we saying you'll be that stupid? Of course not. But why
risk it? Why give your Subconscious a chance to dub Thinwalking
a failure, simply because it's confusing this **get-thin** program with
all the other programs you've ever tried, which are based on **weight
loss**?

To avoid being victimized by that confusion, we can't tell you
strongly enough: get rid of your bathroom scale; give it away or hide
it for a few centuries!

And then turn your attention to the **real** purpose of the Walk
Yourself Thin program, which is to:

Get you thin;

Get you feeling good about your body;

Get you into clothing sizes you always thought were for "other
people;"

Get you loving yourself so you can love others, which is the most important thing in life.

All you need to do is go out every day and put in your miles. You'll soon find that it's the most enjoyable time you spend each day — especially if you have the company of good people or, at the least, a good set of stereo headphones.

Almost without realizing it, you'll start to get thin. Your step will be livelier, the air will smell sweeter, you'll begin **seeking out** your reflection instead of going out of your way to **avoid** it!

Most important: you'll **look forward** to your daily Thinwalking sessions the way you **never** looked forward to day after day of "grapefruit-and-cottage cheese!"

And to make sure you don't jeopardize this wonderful new life by falling victim to the evils lurking in your bathroom scale, we tell you one last time:

Never weigh yourself!

16
The Dawn of a 'New Age'

So, if you're going to get thin, you're going to have to "control" something: either the amount you eat or the amount you exercise.

"Right."

And which is easier to do: "exercising more" or "eating less?"

"Silly question!"

Do you know why?

"No."

Because every fiber of your mind and body has only one goal: to make sure you survive.

And, while **you** might call "half-a-grapefruit-and-black-coffee" a "diet," your mind and body call it "starvation." And since "starvation" is at all times a **threat** to your survival, your mind and body have no choice but to fight it, tooth-and-nail (think back to the last time you went through that kind of "diet" and you'll know how "sharp" those "teeth" and "nails" can be!)

And how do the same mind and body look at the other way of getting thin: "exercise?"

Well, who do you think could flee a lion better: Fatty Arbuckle or Carl Lewis?

Of course!: when survival is on the line, the exercised body will always win out over the non-exercised one.

Your mind and body know this. Which is why, when you start

to exercise, they fall all over themselves to help you: increasing blood flow to the muscles; building muscle at the expense of fat; driving you to exercise by making you "antsy" if you don't; etc.

So when you do finally decide to get thin, you have a choice: try to do it by dieting, and get nothing but a fight from body and soul, or do it by exercising, and get the undying help of those same two guys.
Some choice!

Which is why we can say, without reservation:

THE AGE OF "DIETS" IS OVER!
THE AGE OF "THINWALKING" HAS BEGUN!

"But if exercise is such an odds-on choice for getting thin, why are so many fat people still trying to diet the weight off?"
For one simple reason: because they've been brought up to believe that exercise alone can't possibly burn enough calories to get them thin:

We all know the horror stories: you have to walk or run a whole **mile** to burn off the calories in a pat of butter or an Oreo cookie! And, if those stories were true, the experts would be right: it would take forever to walk off all the butter and cookies in our lives!
But those stories are not true:
Oh sure, you only burn off about a hundred calories for every mile you walk or run. But those hundred calories are only what you burn **while you're walking** (or running)!
What happens after you stop? Does the calorie-burning stop as suddenly as your legs do? Of course not!:

When you walk briskly enough for your walking to be classed as "exercise," you break down a large number of muscle fibers. These broken fibers have to be swept away and new ones built in their place. That takes energy, and lots of it!
You also have to replace the "power molecules" that your walking has used up; **more** "energy" required.
So when all is said and done, you haven't burned just a hundred calories for every mile you've walked — you've burned **two**

hundred or **three** hundred. And taken exercise from being an "impossible" way to get thin to being a very effective way indeed!

Of course, an exercise like Thinwalking still won't give you the "pounds-per-day" losses a good "starvation 'diet'" will — at least for the first day or two of the "diet." But how many people do you know who've taken weight off with that kind of "diet" and kept it off? Or enjoyed doing it?!

Exactly!

And that figure is never going to change — **can't** change — because everything about a "diet" is **anti**-survival while every part of us is **pro**-survival.

Thankfully, with this new knowledge — that exercise alone can burn all the calories we need, to get ourselves thin — we will never have to suffer the horrors of dieting again, but can go, instead, with a "sheer delight:" Thinwalking!

17

Why Thinwalking Works

OK, so the 200 calories I burn during a two-mile walk become 400 by the time you add in all the 'housekeeping' calories. So what? That still can't touch the four **thousand** calories I sock away every day!

"Even if I burn off 400, I'm still 3600 the 'wrong way,' so how can I possibly keep eating like that and still get thin?!"

Very easily:

Let's say that you have, in fact, been averaging 4000 calories a day (and you're right: if you had to depend on exercise to burn off all 4000, the situation would be hopeless: you'd have to walk to Cleveland and back every day, just to "break even!")

But let's see what's really been happening to those "four big ones:"

Say, for example, that you haven't been gaining more than 25 pounds a year (that's a hundred pounds every four years, so be careful before you protest that figure as being "too low").

"Twenty-five pounds a year" is about "two pounds a month."

Since a pound of body fat contains about 3500 calories, that means you've been "gaining" about 7000 calories a month — or a little over 200 calories a day.

Get the picture?:

Regardless what you've been eating every day, **only 200 calories of it is showing up as increased bodysize!**

How can that be, when you've been "packing away" those 4000 calories, day after day? Easy: your daily activities have been burning off the other 3800! (This is not surprising, since it obviously takes more calories to move a heavy body around than it does a light one.)

So you **don't** have to worry about the whole 4000 calories you've been scarfing down! All you have to worry about is the 200 **extra** calories that have been creeping onto your waistline every day!

And how do you get rid of those extra 200?

Well, one mile of Thinwalking will burn off a hundred calories while you're doing it and another hundred or so after you're through, and we've lost our calculator but that sure looks like about 200 from here!

"It's that simple?"

It's that simple:

Walk one mile a day as fast as you comfortably can and you'll bring a "guaranteed 25 pound-a-year weight gain" to a **crashing halt** — without giving up a single cookie!

Want to **lose** 25 pounds a year?

How about Thinwalking **two** miles a day?!

Yes, we hear you:

"'**Two miles**?!' I'm a hundred pounds overweight! I can barely make it from one **room** to another! **Two miles**?!' Why not make it 'two **hundred**?!' Or 'two **thousand**?!'"

The reason we know where you're coming from is because we've just "been there" ourselves. And we know it's hard to believe, but you're going to have to trust us: if you will just get started, walking as fast as you comfortably can for as long as you comfortably can every day, it shouldn't take you more than **two weeks** to get up to those "two miles," no matter how overweight you are at the start and no matter how hard it is for you to put one foot in front of the other.

"Wait a minute: how can that be? How can everyone get to the same point in the same amount of time, no matter where each of them starts?"

We don't know; they all just do!

It's like tearing a sheet of paper: no matter how big the original sheet, nobody you've ever met can manage the "seventh tear" (that is: you tear the original sheet in half, put the two halves on top of each other and tear those two in half and keep doing that until you reach the "seventh tear").

That "seventh tear" becomes the "great equalizer," making the strongest Goliath no mightier than the puniest David.

And that's the way it works with Thinwalking: no matter how heavy you are at the start of those first two weeks, your muscles somehow build themselves up to the point where they can carry you two miles by the end of them.

So don't worry about "making the grade." Your body will give you all the tools you need, to Thinwalk as well as anybody your size ever has.

Just remember one thing: nobody ever got to the **seventh** tear without the **first** one (are your little feet listening??)

18

The Fly in the Ointment

Wait a minute! If all I'm 'putting on' is 200 calories a day, why can't I stop the weight gain by cutting those 200 calories out of my diet? Or turn the **gain** into a **loss** by cutting out the whole **four** hundred?! Why do I have to **exercise** them away?"

Good question; easily answered:

You **can** turn the weight gain into a weight loss by cutting down on what you eat — for a while.

But eventually, this "diet" of yours stops working.

Why?

Because to keep losing weight, your body has to keep pulling fat out of storage; the minute it stops pulling fat out of storage, you stop losing weight.

And why would it stop?

Because the calories the body stores as "fat" are there for "Emergencies Only" — times of real famine, for example, which happened a million years ago and yesterday afternoon in Ethiopia — and, in the long run, anything which doesn't qualify as an "emergency" is just not going to get those calories!

"So what qualifies as an 'emergency?'"
Anything that threatens your survival:

Your body keeps you functioning on two levels: a Lower Level

("Survival") and a Higher Level ("Thrival").

On the Survival Level, the body uses calories to keep your heart beating, your lungs working, and to keep everything else (muscles, brain, body cells) ticking along at "minimum." At the Higher Level, the brain is able to engage in creative thought, the muscles have enough energy for long, hard workouts, etc.

If your body needs, say, 2000 calories to satisfy **both** levels and you give it only 1800, you force it to make a choice: bring those "missing" 200 calories out of storage and keep everything functioning to the "max," or simply withhold those 200 calories from an "unnecessary" (Higher Level) activity and "go with the 1800 you've got."

In the beginning, the body has "no problem" with pulling those missing 200 calories out of storage to keep you humming "on all fours" (and giving you the nifty little weight loss you were shooting for).

But as the shortfall goes on, day after day, the body can't help but think: "Hey: we've got 'starvation' happening here" — and it quickly "shifts gears:"

Suddenly, it stops "wasting" those stored calories on such "foolish" things as "solving problems" and "running a 10 K," and starts holding them back for more important things — like making sure you'll be **alive** next Tuesday!

So your 200-calorie cutback, which got you such a "nice little weight loss" in the beginning, now gets you **nothing**.

So you cut back your eating by **four** hundred calories. But now the body is "on" to you and responds even quicker to your "cutback" with one of its own, so your weight loss stops even sooner this time than it did before.

So you increase your cutback to **eight** hundred calories. And what does your body do? That's right: it finds a way to get along on **eight** hundred fewer calories, and all the fat stays right where it was!

And on and on it goes, with the body matching your every "cutback" with an identical "hold-back" of its own, so the **less** you eat, the **less** fat it pulls out of storage and the **less** weight you lose!

And what is the end result of all your body's "hold-backs?"

Well, since they all come at the expense of Higher Level functions, what you wind up becoming is a near-"zombie," mentally and physically — someone barely able to move, barely able to talk, barely able to think. In other words: someone of no value to his family, his employer, his customers — **anyone**!

And what's worse: someone not losing enough weight to justify a **hundredth** of the torment he's going through!

Kind of cruel of your body to do that to you, especially when you're trying something as noble as getting yourself thin. Unfortunately, your body isn't programmed for "noble;" it's programmed to keep you alive as long as it can and, if you threaten that program by starving yourself, it'll be a cold day in you-know-where before your body will bend over backwards to **help** you!

We would ask you to keep that in mind the next time some new-fangled "diet" comes along that promises it can get around the body's "survival program." If it can, hey: go for it! But if it can't — and there's only about a zillion years of evolution standing in its way — you'd do well to think twice before mortgaging any of your children to go on it!

And while you're doing all this twice-thinking, you might get back to doing what evolution **wants** you to do and (here's a "sneak preview") **WILL release calories** for you to do: walking yourself thin!

19

Why Diets Don't Work

So how does your body feel about you going on a "diet?"

"Hates it!"

And what about your "other half" — that thing living inside your head? How do you think **it** takes to "dieting?"

"Like 'sunburn to sandpaper?'"

Well put!

"Thank you."

Do you know why?

"Same reason, probably."

That's right: "survival."

Do you know why you do everything you do?

"No."

Because a part of your brain called the Subconscious Mind makes you do it (the reason it's called the **Sub**conscious Mind is because it does all its work "behind the scenes," so we're not usually **conscious** of why it's making us do what we do; we just know that it is.)

Like the body, the Subconscious cares about only one thing: your survival. Do something to **threaten** that survival and the Subconscious Mind must stop you, and stop you **good!**

And what could threaten your survival? Well, how about a few months'-worth of "cottage cheese-and-tomato slices?!"

"Sounds yummy!"

Call that a "diet," do you?

"Everyone does."

Well, that's fine. But your Subconscious thinks you've booked passage to Ethiopia, and it's not going to let you rest until you're on the plane home again!

And the longer it takes you to do that, the worse the trip will become.

Until, when you finally do "take off:"

"Gosh, Judy: I didn't know they **made** that many cookies!"

And when you've recovered from your cookie binge, you'll look at your bulbous self in the mirror again and go running out to see what the latest tabloid has to offer:

"Gee," you'll tell your Subconscious, "this one sounds good: 'Papaya-and-pork rinds! Lose a Million Pounds an Hour, Guaranteed!' What do you think, S. C.?"

Believe us: you don't want to know what your "S. C." thinks!

"O. K., I'll buy that: the Subconscious doesn't want me going off the deep end 'diet-wise' — especially 'diets' that are heavy into 'starvation.'

"But what about the other side of the coin — you know, when I'm 'packing away' everything in sight? Where's the old Subconscious then? If it's so interested in my 'survival,' why doesn't it stop me before my calorie count starts to look like the national debt?!

"I mean, even **I** know the effect 'a zillion calories a day' can have on the old 'life span!'"

Exactly. So when your Subconscious lets you go through a salad bar the way Sherman cruised through Georgia, it has nothing to do with ensuring your **physical** survival!

"So, what else?"

The only thing left: **mental** survival.

"Wait a minute! Are you telling me that 'five feet of fudge' is gonna keep me out of the Wacko Ward?"

Your Subconscious thinks it will.

"How?"

Well, what puts you **into** the Wacko Ward?

"Things that make me 'crazy!'"

And what makes you "crazy?"

"When I can't get a 'handle' on things."

Psychologists have a word for that.

"They do?"

Yes. They call it: "anxiety"—

"Oh."

—a feeling of "helplessness."

"Yeah, that's it!"

And what do you do when you get these feelings?

"Well, I go out and eat myself silly."

So you eat to relieve feelings of "helplessness."

"Yeah."

Do you know why?

"No."

We might:

This "anxiety" we're talking about isn't exactly a new item in your life:

When you were a baby, and couldn't get a "handle" on things — when you felt helpless in the face of diaper rash or hunger or being left alone — you did the only thing you could do: you cried.

If you had a good Mommy, and most of us did, she heard your cries and came back into the room.

If you had an Overweight Mommy, as some of us did, or a Mommy who thought her "precious" was always about 20 or 30 seconds away from total starvation anyway, you got fed, no matter why you were crying.

Unfortunately, a lot of the time what you were needing wasn't food, but just some reassurance that Mommy hadn't run off and joined the Space Program while you were in la-la land. When you found out she hadn't, you stopped crying.

But did that stop Mommy?! Not on your life! If your Mommy

was like most Mommies, she just **knew** that the Starvation Patrol was camped outside her door, **itching** to drag her off to jail at the first sign of an undernourished child! So, like it or not, **YOU GOT FED**!

Years later, when a boss or a lover or a term paper is turning "la-la land" into "ca-ca county" and you could use a good dose of Mommy to "right your ship," there will always come a time when you can't **have** Mommy. Which will make you feel about as helpless as you did in that crib of yours.

What to do?

Well, you can't live very long, feeling helpless like that. Your Subconscious knows this, and, since its only purpose is to keep you alive, it knows it has to "do something."

What would work? Obviously: the return of Mommy. But we also know you can't have that, so the Subconscious has to come up with something else.

"What else?"

Well, what always went along with Mommy, every time she came back into the room?

"Mmm: yummy!"

That's right: **food**!

So, as crazy as it might seem, every time you **want** Mommy but can't **have** Mommy, the Subconscious pushes you toward the next best thing: food!

And is it the "next best thing?"

Oh sure!:

No better way to get back on your boss's "A-list" than by eating five or six dozen cookies!

Want to lure your lover back into the nest? No problem: just drown yourself in hot fudge sundaes! That always works!

And how about that term paper: why bust a gut doing research for it, when 15 or 20 Snickers bars can do it for you?!

Right!

And the really sad part is not that the food doesn't solve anything — after all, what could cold, dead candy bars do for you that the warmest, most **alive** creatures on Earth have trouble doing? — but that the foods the Subconscious gets you to eat are almost always the kind you can't **stop** eating once you've started (sugary; salty; buttery; etc.)

So not only does the Subconscious Mind's "solution" do nothing to relieve the **original** anxiety, it gives you a whole **new** anxiety to worry about: "overweight," and the social rejection that automatically goes with it!

And how does the Subconscious handle that new anxiety?

How else?: more food!

Until you wind up doing nothing but you-know-what!

And what happens if you decide to "turn the tables" on the the Subconscious — tell it that you won't be "buying" its "solution" anymore; that you'll be going on a "diet" instead?

Well, think back to the **last** time you went on a "diet" and try to remember what kind of cooperation your Subconscious gave you (and they say pain has no memory! Right!)

So, what to do?

Easy:

Don't tell your Subconscious you won't be "buying" its "solution!" **Don't** go on a "diet!" **Don't** do anything that will make your Subconscious "get its back up!"

If it thinks you need a thousand cookies to "survive," give it a thousand cookies! Don't keep forcing it to go overnight from a "thousand cookies" to "grapefruit-and-cottage cheese," because it'll never do it!

But, while you're giving in to its **mental** demands, just remember one thing:

The same Subconscious that needs you to eat has **absolutely no need for you to be fat**!

That's right: as far as the Subconscious is concerned, as long as it gets you eating those cookies — and thereby "saving" you **mentally** — it could care less what those cookies are doing to you **physically**!

So what?

So take advantage of that "loophole!" Eat every cookie the Subconscious wants you to eat. Then go out and walk them all off! **Your Subconscious won't stop you**!

And what will that do — eating cookies, then walking them off? Nothing much: just keep your Subconscious deliriously happy and out of your "life," so that you can work at making that "life" as deliriously happy as your Subconscious!

If, somewhere down the line, you can convince your Subconscious that it's been way off base all these years with its "food solution," terrific! But if you can't, no problem: you can get still get thin and fit in the **face** of its mistake, by walking yourself thin.

So do it. Get off your kiester, go out and get thin!

Don't ever worry about what you're eating or why you're eating it, because you don't have to!

If you **can** control your eating without "tipping off" your Subconscious, do it: it can only make your Thinwalking that much more effective.

But if you can't, **forget it**! Just go out and Thinwalk every day and you'll solve more problems than you ever thought possible — or knew you had!

20
"...from the Black Lagoon"

We're all "creatures of habit:"

Know of anybody who doesn't get hungry for the same breakfast/lunch/dinner/snacks at the same times every day?

How about you smokers: find it easy to make a phone call or start your car without lighting up first?!

And you "5:30 drinkers:" Think it would be easy to simply do without one day, when that time rolls around?! Yeah, tell me about it!

And what about you guys who put your right shoe on before your left: go ahead and do it the other way round for a change and see how "comfortable" it makes you feel!

No: the list of things we do out of habit is virtually endless.

What's **not** so endless, though, is the list of reasons **why** we do these things.

In fact, it stops at "one:" "survival."

"Wait a minute:"

What?

"You're telling me that the smoking driver **needs** to light up — to 'survive?!'"

Well, yes and no—

"And the 5:30 boozer: you expect me to believe that alcoholics have a better survival record than **non**-alcoholics?!"

No, I don't.

"Then what exactly are you talking about?!"

I'm talking about what it **seems** we need, to survive!

"This better be good!"

It is:

Every day, two things happen: 1) You do a lot of stuff; 2) You make it to the next day.

The Subconscious "sees" both of those and thinks that the stuff you did was the **reason** you made it through!

Since its only job is to make sure you're around tomorrow, that would seem to simplify things:

If what you did yesterday got you to today, what better way to get you to tomorrow than to make you do those same things all over again — no matter how absurd or destructive those things might be (the Subconscious makes no judgment about whether an action is "good" or "bad;" if you did it and survived, it thinks you **needed** to do it to survive and it's going to get you doing it all over again until you tell it to stop!)

And how does it get you doing the same things all over again?

By setting off the physical "fireworks" that make you "hunger" to do those things and drive you crazy if you **don't** (stomach churning; a "longing" in your gut; heart palpitations; etc.)

So, go ahead: have a jelly donut at 9:30 today and 9:30 tomorrow and see what happens to you, along about 9:30 on the third day!

That's right: You'll crave that jelly donut as if your life depended on it!

Because, to your Subconscious, **it does**!

So what?

So, if your life really **did** depend on that jelly donut, you'd be a fool to ignore your craving for it; that's called "starvation!"

But the cold truth is: your life **doesn't** depend on that jelly donut; it only **seems** to, because the Subconscious uses the exact same "machinery" to get us satisfying **its** "survival" needs as the body uses to signal **real** hunger!

So what?

So, you can ignore as many of these "false hungers" as you want, without worrying that you're causing yourself any harm by doing so.

And what will ignoring these false demands do for you?

Well, in the same way you "train" your Subconscious to get you hungering for a jelly donut at 9:30 by **having** jelly donuts at 9:30, you can "train" your Subconscious to **stop** making you hunger for jelly donuts at 9:30 by **not** having them for a day or two!

And as it happens: after you've put out the "fire below" by doing without something for a few days, you usually have trouble remembering why you thought that something was such a "life-and-death proposition" in the first place!

Do you **have** to put out the "fire below?"

No.

As long as you walk off all those unnecessary jelly donuts, you'll still get thin.

It's just that it doesn't take a genius to realize that if you **can** do without some of those extra calories, you can only **help** your walking program!

And, if you do want to do without them, knowing that you only crave them out of **habit**, not out of any real **need**, should make your job that much easier.

So if you want to tackle your eating habit, to help your Thinwalking, you now have one of the primary tools for doing so. If you don't, no problem: just keep on walking!

And who knows: if you Thinwalk at 5:30 today and then again at 5:30 tomorrow and 5:30 the next day, maybe your Subconscious will do for Thinwalking what it so easily does for donuts and beer: make it a _____!

21
Wrapping it Up

So now you have the whole picture:

• When you could use a little human companionship but can't get it, your Subconscious Mind pushes you toward the "next best thing:" food;

• The food doesn't solve the problem—in fact, makes it worse — but it's the only "solution" the Subconscious Mind has, so it keeps pushing it on you;

• Most of the foods the Subconscious gets you to eat are chemically addictive — "sugary;" "salty;" "buttery" — so you keep eating them long after the psychological reasons for doing so have vanished;

• The Subconscious remembers what you ate on any given day and notices that you survived to the next day. It then "connects" those two things and thinks that all it has to do, to get you to tomorrow, is make you eat, today, exactly the way you ate yesterday. Until eating that way becomes impossible **not** to do; becomes, in other words: a "habit."

Breaking this incredibly complex eating cycle — which is what all "diets" try to do — is a monumental task, and one that is better left for another time and place, especially since we don't need to break it to get thin.

For now, just keep it in the back of your mind as you "suggest" to your Subconscious that it make your daily **Thinwalk** an "impossible thing not to do;" something along the lines of a... "habit!"

22

The Magic of Thinwalking

So how does the Subconscious feel about "dieting?"
"Hates it!"
—And your body?
"Same way!"
You know why?
"I'm waiting..."

The body's main function, for the last 20 million years or so, has been to get you to distant hunting grounds, where you can run after a buffalo, kill the buffalo, and somehow get the buffalo back to your cave.

That you now need a computer to even **spell** "buffalo" is irrelevant! As far as your body is concerned, you could be hunting the big guys tomorrow and it has to be ready for you, in the same way that your great-great-...-great grandfather's body was "ready!"

And what does it mean to "be ready?"

First of all, it means that your body has chosen fat for storing most of its energy, rather than the starch that plants use, because, at 9 calories of energy per gram of fat (vs. the 4 of starch) you more than double your chances of getting to the hunting grounds and back.

Second, it means that your body is programmed to **conserve** your fat stores when something threatens them, since it has to be sure it can always "buy" you that round-trip ticket to "buffaloville."

Nothing wrong with all that — after all, it's the reason you're here to read these words — except when you go on a "diet." Then, you wish your body had never **heard** of a buffalo!:

What was a "good thing" — fat being able to squeeze so many calories in such a little space — now becomes a "bad thing," since you have to deny yourself an "ocean" of calories to get rid of a "teacup" of fat.

And that's just for the **first** "teacup!" By the time you're going for "Teacup Number Two," your body has already shifted into "Conservation Overdrive" and you have to turn your back on **two** oceans of calories to get the same results! Then **three** "oceans;" then **four**. Until you wind up doing without a whole **world**ful of calories to get rid of a "thimbleful" of blubber!

And what does your life look like, along about "thimble time?"

Just great!: you're weak as a kitten, irritable as Scrooge, trying to remember how your shoes are tied, and looking like you're doing an all-day "step test" with your bathroom scale, hoping the darn thing will register **something** that'll make it all worthwhile!

When it doesn't, you throw up your hands and come down with an ice cream cone in each one, which instantly whisks your mind and body out of "Dieter's Hell!"

Which is where you remain.

Until the next "miracle 'diet'" comes along that wonders why you're worrying about something as silly as a billion years of evolution!

At which point, it's "off to the races" again — with each new "race" somehow ending up closer and closer to the front door of Divorce Court!

Of course, there's really no need to **fight** evolution when trying to get thin, because it's so easy to get evolution's **help**!

How?

By getting thin in a way where we work **with** Nature, rather than **against** her: **using** calories rather than **restricting** them.

In other words: "exercising" rather than "dieting."

Why is it that your body views exercising as such a Godsend? Because exercised muscles are survival muscles, and your body loves the sound of that word!

And how does your body show its love?

Quite simply: the same body that so zealously **guarded** its stored calories when using them would **threaten** survival, now sends them forth **gladly**, since doing so **increases** your chances of making it through.

And what is the end result of all this sending forth?

Of course: easy and permanent slimness!

And that's what gives Thinwalking a power, a "magic," that no "diet" could ever possess:

Every time you Thinwalk, you break down a unit's-worth of muscle; the body then releases a unit's-worth of fat to help rebuild that unit of muscle. This makes you one unit **stronger** on Day Two than you were on Day One!

Every time you Thinwalk, you use up a unit's-worth of glycogen to fuel the walk; the body then releases another unit of fat to replace the glycogen. This "glycogen burn" makes you one unit **lighter** on Day Two than you were on Day One!

Get the picture?:

Every "unit" you walk uses up **two** "units" of fat;

Every "unit" you walk makes you one unit stronger and one unit lighter, so you can walk **one unit faster and one unit farther** on Day Two than you could on Day One!

In other words, everywhere you look, Thinwalking is giving you a "two-for-one" exchange!

And what kind of "exchange" does a "diet" give you? Well, when you deny your body a unit's-worth of calories, the most it can do is burn up a unit's-worth of stored fat to make up the difference. That's it: no new muscle, no glycogen replacement — nothing! Just a "one-for-one" exchange — and then, only if you're real lucky!

And because of the way it works, not only is Thinwalking a more **efficient** way to get thin than "dieting" could ever be, it also has the wonderful "side effect" of making you look **forward** to each lost inch — not cringe at the thought of what it's going to take to lose it!

One more thing: when you "diet" yourself thin, all you're doing is emptying out your fat stores. So, when an excess calorie sneaks into your body — and it will — it has only one place to go: those fat stores.

When you **walk** yourself thin, on the other hand, you build these enormous "metabolic furnaces" in your legs, known as "muscles." Now, when that excess calorie gets past your watchful eye, it has a **choice** of places to go: it can get **stored** in the fat pad, like before, or it can get **burned** in the muscle and vanish forever.

"So is that what Thinwalking guarantees — that none of those extra calories will ever turn to fat?"

No. Thinwalking just gives them a **chance** not to be turned into fat — which is a lot more than they get on your typical "diet!"

So your choice is clear: try to "diet" yourself thin and watch yourself get weaker and meaner each day, with every extra calorie you eat turning instantly to fat. Or walk yourself thin and grow stronger and more alive as your body gets smaller and smaller, while you at least give all those extra calories a **chance** to get burned, rather than stored!

As we've already said: some choice!

Which is why we can again proclaim it:

THE AGE OF "DIETS" IS OVER!
THE AGE OF "THINWALKING" HAS BEGUN!

— and welcome you to that magical New Age!

23

"Can we Talk?"

The fact is: unless you deliberately sabotage it, Thinwalking will get you thin and keep you thin.

"Why would I sabotage it?"

Because being thin is a lot different than being fat:

1) Instead of turning away from you, people will now turn toward you and want to interact with you. Which means you're going to have to interact with them. You can't rely on your fat pad to keep them away anymore, because it won't be there anymore.

2) People will start giving you things to do that they would entrust only to people who are psychologically mature (which obese people definitely are not), so you'll have to start acting more like an adult.

3) By getting thin, you'll be treated with love, respect and admiration by everyone you meet.

Nothing wrong with that, except you've been told, all your life, that you were unworthy of such feelings. This will set up a conflict between what is happening to you and what people in your past — parents and others — told you could never happen.

So you'll be tossed between the good feelings you're getting from being thin, and the bad feelings you're getting from proving that all those wonderful people were dead wrong all these years; in other words, that your "infallible" mommy or daddy were not so infallible after all, which starts to make you uneasy about a lot of other things they told you!

And, since no one likes to be ill-at-ease, we get the sad situation of newly-thin people putting back all their lost bodysize, just to prove that mommy and daddy were right about everything all along!

All we can say is: mommies and daddies do the best they can. But if someone gave **them** bad information along the way, that's all they can pass on to you.

So don't stop getting thin, or go back to being fat, just because someone has told you: "You're not good enough to be thin!"

Believe me: You're good enough! We all are!

And as for the first two things: interacting with people and acting more like an adult: if you had to do them overnight, we wouldn't hold out much hope for you; no one could change that quickly. But the fact is, you **won't** have to do them overnight, because you aren't going to get **thin** overnight.

Most likely, it will take you a year or more to get as thin as you should be, which means you'll have a year or more to learn to act like a thin person; and no one has ever failed to do so, given that amount of time to learn.

So just relax, do your Thinwalking, lose your bodysize and, before you know it, the world will be yours — no matter **what** you've been told!

24
"Watch Out!"

We skirted the issue in the last chapter, so we'll "unskirt" it now:

When you get thin, you're going to "tick" some people off. Which people?

The ones who need a certain predictability to their lives, to feel secure.

It doesn't matter to these people whether the predictable things are good or bad — just that they're predictable.

They find comfort, for example, in the thought that "Nothing's surer than death and taxes" — even though it deals with two of the most dreaded things we humans face — because of the certainty, the predictability, of "death" and "taxes."

And what happens to these people when one of their predictable things changes?

Of course: they start to feel like the wheels are coming off!

Which is exactly what happens when they see you get thin:

One of the things they could **always** count on, like "death" and "taxes," was your being obese. It allowed them to get all their ducks in a row each day.

Then suddenly, you're not obese anymore! You're not the social reject they could always count on you being.

How do you think they're going to take that? Do you think your new physique is going to make them feel **better** about things — **more** secure? Or is it going to threaten the very foundation on which their lives are built?!

Of course.

And how are they going to react to having their lives made **less** predictable, **less** secure? Are they going to congratulate you on a "job well done?" Or are they more likely to express some concern, perhaps,

that your weight-loss program is "hurting your health;"

that you've been looking a little ill lately, like you "need some food;"

that now that you're thin, you can "stop this 'insanity'" and go back to living a "normal" life (i.e., your "normal" 5-10,000 calories per day!);

that you've got a lot of money invested in your (oversized) wardrobe, and "are you really getting the most out of that investment, now that you're thin?";

—and on and on, with one good reason after another why you should return to your former, fat self!

Why are they doing all this?

Of course: for your own good!

Yeah, right!

All we can say is, "Watch out!" We hope and pray you have none of these people in your life. But if you do: "Watch out!"

While it may seem evil for them to be pushing you back to a life that brought you nothing but misery, you must understand that they **have** to do it, that if they didn't, **their** world would be threatened, and they can't let that happen!

Don't for a minute, though, buy the nonsense about them doing it for your own good! That's the **last** thing on their minds and if you fall for it, shame on **you**!

Instead, just nod your head when they make their earnest suggestions and promise to give those suggestions your "strongest consideration" in the "very near future!"

And then go out and Thinwalk another 5, 10 miles, to increase the "security" of your **own** world — that's right: the one **you** have to live in!

25
Goals

Universal Truth:

People who set goals and work toward them are more successful than people who don't.

Everyone's goal, of course, should be: to live the best life possible.

And even though people will differ on what the "best life possible" would include, no one would argue that being fat, and having difficulty doing the simple things that are "no problem" for thin people, could ever be a part of it.

So, if you're a fat person, the one goal you **must** work toward, to have any **hope** of living an optimal life, is: getting thin.

And how do you reach that **big** goal?

Of course: by achieving a **little** goal every day: "Walking as fast as you comfortably can for as long as you comfortably can."

If you can just do that, then achieving the long-term goal — getting thin — will become automatic, and will put you within easy reach of your overall goal: living the best life possible.

We hate to make it sound so simple, but that's what it is. All Thinwalking asks is that you take some responsibility for your own destiny, and do it for at least one hour out of every 24.

If you can do that, your "race" is won! If you can't, you'd better read the next chapter.

26
Control

How do you feel about "self-control?"

"Hate it!"

Much more fun to be **out** of control, isn't it: smoking and drinking and eating everything in sight?!"

"Absolutely!"

But it would still be nice to get thin, wouldn't it?

"Why do you think I'm here?!"

So, you don't want to control yourself—

"Right."

—but you want to get thin.

"Also right."

And you really think you can do one without the other?

"I don't know, but I'll probably die trying!"

Maybe we can stop you a few steps short of the grave!

First of all, it really is a fact of nature: if you're going to get thin, you're going to have to change **something**! If you don't want to reduce the amount you eat, then you're going to have to increase the amount you exercise. There's no getting around it.

"Oh, poop!"

But all is not lost.

"It's not?"

No. Because when you finally stop trying to "diet" yourself

thin and turn to exercise, you hit the "mother lode:"

Instead of having to control yourself **24** hours a day, which is what you have to do on every "diet," you only have to "control" yourself **one** hour a day, to get the same or better results!

What you do with the other 23 hours is your business, as long as you don't eat **more** than you normally would!

This, of course, is nothing short of a miracle!:

Instead of asking people who've never been able to control their eating for 24 **minutes** to suddenly control it for 24 **hours**, all they have to do is **trade** one of those eating hours for an hour of Thinwalking.

(Actually, there's nothing to stop you from eating **while** you Thinwalk; you just have to be careful not to spill any of the salad, or choke on the cookie crumbs. And it's a lot easier to cut up the steak **before** you start walking!)

If you will just "control" yourself that one hour a day, you can do whatever you want (within obvious limits) the other 23, and still get as thin as it's possible to get.

Of course, there are some fat folk who are so infantile that they have to be out of control **every** hour of the day. For them, of course, there are no miracles and never will be.

For the rest of you, we ask only that you set aside one hour a day to do something that, after you get over your initial soreness, will be one of the most enjoyable hours you spend each day.

If you can do that — if you can give Thinwalking that hour — all your prayers for slimness — voiced and otherwise — will finally be answered !

If you can't, you'd better keep praying!

27
"The Best Thing"

The flip side of our need for goals is our need for achievements; without them, we are little more than plant life.

Unfortunately, most of us are so busy earning a living in a routine way that we don't get many chances to pile up such achievements.

That's where Thinwalking can help:

No matter how bad or insignificant our days may otherwise be, Thinwalking is always there to make sure we have at least one shining moment we can point to; it is the one thing we can rely on to make us better off today than we were yesterday: more fit; less fat; happier; more alive!

It is this sense of achievement that sets Thinwalking apart from every other get-thin program — this feeling that you are, in **every** way, a better person today than you were yesterday, and that you've gotten there by doing something **positive** — "exercise" — rather than something **negative**: "starvation."

That is why Thinwalking is an almost-impossible habit to break, why Thinwalkers would rather give up **anything** than their daily Thinwalk:

Today they walk six miles; tomorrow they'll shoot for seven! When they started, they could barely move; now they're a blur!

Before Thinwalking, their lives were miserable; now they're a joy!

And the nicest thing about these "miracles" is that they're so easily gotten: all you have to do is put one foot in front of the other, as fast as you comfortably can for as long as you comfortably can.

Of course, if you have something better to do during that hour, something that will make your spirits soar equally as high, far be it from us to take you away from that.

But if you don't — if you could use an extra dose of "accomplishment" — why not join us on the street, in the park, at the track?

We'd love to have you!

And you know something? So would you!

28

"...and twice on Sundays!"

You say I should Thinwalk every day."

That's right.

"But some days, I can barely move. Am I really doing myself any good, dragging my butt around the neighborhood for all of five minutes?!"

Physically, no. But otherwise — yes:

Your goal, for anything good that you do, should be to make it a habit.

Why?

So you just do it automatically, which guarantees it'll get done.

And how do you make something a habit?

Just one way: by doing it over and over again.

Which is why you should go for a walk every day, even if they need a time-lapse camera to tell if you're moving!

One other reason:

As we've already said: you often don't know, at the start of a walk, how good you'll feel five or ten minutes into it. And if you don't give it a shot, you'll **never** know! So that's why you should at least

try to walk every day!

If, after giving it your all for those five or ten minutes, you really don't have it, then quit; things aren't going to get any better and you're only fooling yourself if you think they will.

Remember, there's always "tomorrow." Just make sure "tomorrow" really **is** "tomorrow," and not "today."

To do that, test it; try to walk. If it's "not there," it's "not there!" But at least try!

Every day!

29

"To Your Health!"

Was that your bumper sticker we saw?

"Which one?"

"SO MANY COOKIES; SO LITTLE TIME?"

"Yeah, that's mine! You like it?!"

Real cute! And we were going to talk to you about "health!"

"So — talk away!"

But—

"Look: I love my cookies. But I've been thinking..."

Yes?

"You know those charts you sent me?"

From the insurance company?

"Right! Well, I finally looked at them last night."

And?

"Well, they got me thinking: maybe those cookies **aren't** my 'best friend.' Maybe I **could** use a change."

We've all seen the charts. What they tell you is that, everything else being equal, thin people live a lot longer than fat people.

But what those charts **don't** tell you is: all else being equal, **exercised** thin people live a lot longer than **anybody**!

So what?

Well, we know there are two ways to get thin: dieting and exercise.

When you diet yourself thin, all you do is empty out your fat stores; you do nothing to challenge the organs that can give you a longer, healthier life: your heart, lungs and blood vessels!

When you **walk** yourself thin, on the other hand, you get those "health builders" working for you from the very first step, so that, by the time you're down to your proper body size, that body is not just "unfat" — it's **fit!**

Which means you get a "double bonus" from Thinwalking: not only is it **easier** to get thin (you're not fighting your Subconscious all the time), you're also **healthier** when you get there!

Of course, all you really have to do, to make up your mind about which way to go (dieting versus exercise), is look at the **glorious** face of someone who has walked himself thin and compare it to the **"death-warmed-over"** face of someone who has tried to do the same thing by dieting!

The minute you do that, there will be only one thing left to say:

"Welcome to the World of Thinwalking!"

30
Other Exercises

Obviously, Thinwalking is an exercise program, and is the only physical exercise you will ever need, to get as thin as your Creator would like you to be.

However, there are other "exercises" you could be doing, in between Thinwalking sessions, that aren't exactly "physical," but that can help keep you on the Thinwalking track.

Exercise 1: Look at Fat People

Take every opportunity you can to look at fat people (in America, unfortunately, we have plenty of opportunities!)

How do they look to you: Good? Attractive? Happy? Graceful? Healthy?

Or do they look, to you, the way they look to everyone else: sad? repulsive?

Is that really the way **you** want to look? Because, if you're as fat as them, that **is** the way you look, like it or not!

You **don't** like it? Then why not do something about it! Something like making Thinwalking as much a part of your daily routine as eating.

Before you know it, your excess bodysize will begin to vanish, and you will soon be the "subject" of Exercise 2.

Exercise 2: Look at Thin People

This, of course, is just the flip side of Exercise 1. And it's just as important.

How do thin people look to you? Good, huh? Attractive! Sexy! Graceful! Happy! Healthy! Able to buy and wear nice clothes, not retooled army tents!

Do you look like that? Don't you want to?

If you do, see "Exercise 1."

While it sounds like we're being "flip" with these two "exercises," we're not: We want you to look long and hard at every fat person you meet. Look at them until you no longer want to be one of them.

Similarly with thin people: look at them; admire them; imagine what it would be like to be like them. Watch them get into and out of a chair; watch them walk across a room — effortlessly.

Yes: there are mean thin people; there are unhappy thin people.

Thinness is no **guarantee** of happiness; all thinness does is eliminate the **un**happiness of being fat.

But to achieve happiness of **any** kind, you first have to get rid of all **un**happiness. And if getting thin does that, then you have to get thin — which is easy to do, by walking yourself thin.

And to remind you **why** you're Thinwalking, do the above two "exercises" every day, until **you** are the one the fatties look longingly at!

31
A Way Out

One of the nicest things about getting thin is that, if you don't like it, you can always get fat again! You're not trapped in some "jackpot" you can't get out of:

The cookie and candy companies will still be in business; salad bars will still be doling out "zillion-calorie-a-spoonful" dressings; you can still get as many Big Macs-and-fries as your pocketbook will allow!

All we ask is that you at least give yourself a chance to see what life is like as a thin person; how much easier it is to interact with people, interact with your environment, interact with **yourself**!

If all the joys that go with being thin don't happen to suit you, no problem: get fat again! No one's going to stop you!

Just do us a favor and give Thinwalking a whole-hearted try. Once you do, we think you'll discover what so many before you have discovered:

The only truly happy people are thin people or those on their way to becoming thin.

Any reason not be one of **them** for a change?!

32
Christmas

With the Walk Yourself Thin program, every day is "Christmas," especially if you've been able to add a bit of reduced eating to your Thinwalking:

You can't wait to get up in the morning and put your clothes on, to find out how much looser they are today than they were the day before (remember: You'll never be able to **see** any change in body size from day to day, so don't expect to).

You admire yourself from as many angles as you can; you can't get enough of yourself.

That's OK: don't be embarrassed by it. You deserve it. You've earned it. It's normal.

Never forget one thing: The purpose of this program is to get you loving yourself. No one, in the history of the world, has ever been able to truly love someone else without loving himself first. And the first step toward loving yourself is loving your **physical** self — your body.

So go ahead! Love it; touch it; stroke it; feel how good it feels and imagine how good it's going to feel when every last drop of blubber has been used up by your getting-delicious leg muscles!

One piece of advice, though: always save the clothing you were wearing when you started the Thinwalking program.

Why?

Because, as you keep looking at yourself each "every-day-is-Christmas" morning, you may seem to get bigger and bigger before your very eyes, until, after a few minutes of looking, you decide that there has been, in fact, no change from the day before, and you start to get disappointed — forgetting, of course, that we've told you all along to expect no change from one day to the next.

If this does happen to you, go to your closet and haul out those extra-large clothes that you were barely getting into when you began Thinwalking. Put them on. **Now** look at yourself.

If seeing the overall progress you've made since you began doesn't cure your disappointment, nothing will!

Trust us: it will!

And you can just relax and go back to enjoying "Christmas morning!"

33
For the Few

When I was in junior high school, I had a friend — Stan — who had as perfect a physique as you could possibly have (eventually, Stan "used" this physique to become a superb long-distance runner).

I, on the other hand, had the worst body in the history of the school — 50-60 pounds overweight at all times — and the only physical activity I ever got was lighting up as many cigarettes as I could steal from my mother's purse!

How Stan and I got to be friends I'll never know, except that a lot of mothers would tell their sons: "Go hang out with Rives! He may be a degenerate slob, but he's also very bright, and it wouldn't hurt your report card if a little of that 'brightness' rubbed off on you!" — and I think that's what was going on here.

Anyway, not only did Stan and I have different bodies, we had different **attitudes** toward our bodies:

Whereas I saw nothing wrong with the way I looked and couldn't wait for lunch (where I'd race through my own meal, so I'd have time to polish off everyone else's), Stan was always on a "diet:" starving himself the minute he could pinch a microscopic bit of fat around his middle (I tried to tell him that what he was pinching was what most people called "skin," but he wouldn't hear of it!)

The upshot of the story is that Fat David kept getting fatter and fatter, while Skinny Stan never gained an ounce his entire life.

Why do I mention this?

For one reason:

This book was written to help very fat people — people like myself. And yet, I know who'll be buying it and getting the most benefit from it: the "Stans" of this world — those folks who've suddenly found themselves ten, twenty pounds overweight and "won't rest" until they're rid of them!

However, on the off chance that one of you very fat people has stumbled upon this book and hasn't yet tossed it aside — with a "Why would I need this?" — we dedicate this chapter to you.

Having recently been a nifty 100 pounds overweight myself, I know what you're up against when someone says, "Go — walk yourself thin:" at that size, I couldn't walk five **feet**, never mind "**thin!**"

In fact, if someone had asked me if I had any working muscles in those tree trunks hanging from my hips, I would have wondered what planet he was from!

And yet, even though I could barely move, I knew that Thinwalking held the answer to all my prayers: getting thin without giving up any of the foods I lived for.

So off I went, to "walk myself thin."

And how did I do the first day?

You got it: I walked five feet — and did it in well under a minute!

The second day I did much better: **ten** feet (unfortunately, I left my watch at home, so I don't know how long it took me. Over a minute, I reckon, but definitely less than two).

The third day, I managed what seemed like 50 or 60 feet — to the end of my block and back. Of course, that stretch is slightly uphill, so it was the same as if I'd walked a **hundred** feet on level ground (Frank Shorter: look out!)

Anyway, there I was: Three full days into the program and still going nowhere!

So what finally happened?

Well, to make a long story short:

Two weeks later, I was coasting my way through two **miles** (that's right: "**miles**!");

A week after that, I managed to do four miles in under an hour (not **far** under; just "under!");

Another two weeks and I was doing five miles in that same hour!

As I write this, I'm looking to get my time for a "10K" (6.2 miles) down to a "respectable" level (around an hour).

The point is: what if I had given up after that first day? or the second? or the third? Where would I be now, except for the obvious: 100 size-pounds overweight?

Where I would be is: someone in the same old rut, doing nothing to get himself out of that rut.

The question is: Is that really any way to live — to be doing nothing to make your life better — especially when something like Thinwalking can do it so easily?

So my advice to you very fat people is:

1) Get started
2) Don't give up.

I don't care if you only do the same five feet I did on Day One. As long as you do those five feet as fast as you comfortably can, you'll be Thinwalking:

You'll be using some glycogen from your muscles (which will have to be replaced) and you'll be tearing down some muscle fibers (which will have to be rebuilt). And to do both of those things, your body will have to take fat from wherever it's stored.

And every time the glycogen gets replaced and the muscles get rebuilt, you'll be able to walk faster and faster and farther and farther, until you're walking distances and speeds you thought I was only joking about!

All you have to do is get started. Don't worry how far or how fast you're going. Just get out there and Thinwalk every day.

Soon, you'll forget how painful it was to move those first five feet! Soon, you'll realize you **do** have muscles inside those "tree trunks," and they feel **good** when you use them!

(If they **don't** feel good on a particular day, that's because the glycogen **hasn't** all been replaced and the muscle fibers **haven't** all been rebuilt [after all: just because you want them to be doesn't mean they will be, especially if you're in your "middle years."]

(Not to worry: just walk as fast and as far as your "healing" legs will comfortably take you. The next session, or the one after that, will find you bounding around like a gazelle again, so who cares what happened the day before?!)

And soon after you've started your Thinwalking program, you'll wake up to find that your clothes are falling off you. And you'll have "no choice" but to go out and buy a size smaller.

And you'll be very nonchalant around the salesperson, and with all the people you meet on the way home, where you'll slam the door behind you, "leap" into your new clothes and dash to the mirror to see how you look!

Which will be: "Terrific!"

And the week after that? "**More** terrific!"

And the week after that? "So good I can't **stand** it!"

It's all possible and it's all so easy.

All you have to do is get started and your dreams of getting thin will finally come true.

Take it from me, who used to be you.

34

Going on a "Diet"

So you know how senseless it is to go on a "diet."

"Absolutely!"

So what will you do, sometime during the next year?

"Go on a 'diet.'"

Do you know why?

"Because I'm fat?"

No, because you're infantile.

"I beg your pardon!"

Don't be upset: all abusive eaters are; it comes with the territory.

"Oh."

And if there's one thing that all infantile people have in common, it's a belief in magic. And since that's what most "diets" promise — **"Lose 10 Pounds in 5 Minutes!"** — they're right up your alley!

Unfortunately, you probably **will** lose ten pounds in the first five minutes!

"I will?!"

Yes — all of it "water." But that won't matter: you'll step off the scale thinking you've finally arrived in "'diet' Heaven" (forgetting, of course, that those are the exact same results that all the "'diets' from Hell" ever gave you!)

And you'll order a new wardrobe and cancel your life insurance and begin making all sorts of plans for the Wonderful New You.

Until the magic "goes south" in the **second** five minutes and you never lose another ounce!

"What happened?"

Nothing special. You just read the headline wrong. You thought it said: "Lose 10 Pounds **Every** 5 Minutes!"

Since that's impossible — we humans wouldn't have lasted this long if fat were that easy to lose — you're right back where you started: slogging your guts out to drop an ounce or two a week!

Before you go on your next "slog," try this:

Think of your overweight as a redwood tree that you're trying to chop down.

There are two ways to chop down any tree:

- An inch at a time
- With one mighty blow.

If I were the tree and I knew that the only way you'd consider me properly felled is with a single stroke, I'd be real happy about things, since I'd know that what you were asking would require something called "magic," and there "ain't no such thing!"

On the other hand, if you had a sudden change of heart and could live with chopping me down an inch at a time, I'd know my goose was cooked, since my only defense against you — that there is no "magic" — would now be completely useless!

When it comes to chopping down your redwood (getting thin), Thinwalking is of the "'one-inch-at-a-time' school;" all the "miracle 'diets,'" fasting programs, etc., are of the "one-fell-swoop" variety, and you'd do real well to stick a rabbit up your sleeve before you go on one!

Will knowing that such programs rely strictly on magic to get you thin stop you from pursuing them? Of course not:

Has telling people that the odds against winning the lottery are 14 million-to-one ever stopped anyone from playing it?! Not on your life!

An infant is an infant, and nothing, short of a million years of psychoanalysis, is going to change that. As far as you're concerned, there's a "magical" way that impossible things can become possible and you're going to keep searching for it till you find it!

Fine! Search for it! It's **fun** being an infant! If it weren't, no adult would ever be one!

But while your "magical" self keeps bouncing off the "redwood," no matter how promising an "axe" it uses, you might try slipping your **non**-magical self a cute little "hatchet" called "Thinwalking" for an hour or so each day and let it whittle your "tree" down an inch at a time!

That way, it won't matter if your magical "axe" never does what it promised to do; your "tree" will be gone and you can **tell** people it did!

So do us that one favor:

While you're waiting around for some magic to happen, don't pass up the guaranteed results that Thinwalking can provide, as "unmagical" as those might be!

And when you do decide to "go for the 'magic,'" never forget that it's virtually impossible to lose weight by "miracle" programs alone — since they're all based on varying degrees of starvation, and the **more** you starve your body, the **less** fat it brings out of storage; so the only hope your "**diet**" has of getting you thin, after the first day or two, is whatever **exercise** you're doing along with it!

A word of warning, though:

If your new "diet" makes you so weak or so discouraged that you want to give up on **all** weight-reduction programs — Thinwalking included — abandon that "diet" immediately, so you won't be throwing out a very healthy "baby" (Thinwalking) with some very sorry "bathwater!"

Aside from that: "diet" away! See if you really **can** live on "papayas-and-prune juice" the rest of your life; maybe there **is** some weight-loss magic in paying twenty dollars for a bowl of dehydrated soup, or going without solid food for a couple of decades, or "exchanging" a piece of cheese for two apples!

But while you're jumping from one screwball program to another, don't forget one thing: Thinwalking, all by itself, will get you thin, and do it the way Nature intended. It may take what you consider a long time (1-2 years, depending on how overweight you are), but after all: the weight went **on** an ounce at a time, so what could be more "natural" than to take it off the same way?!

Some people, of course, prefer that "guaranteed ounce" to a "pipedream pound!"

Those people are called "adults," and adults don't believe in magic.

What do **you** believe in?!

35

"If you can..."

Why is Thinwalking so successful?

"Because you don't have to change the way you eat."

Good. But what if you **could** change the way you eat?

"Then you'd probably be even **better** off!"

Exactly: Thinwalking burns fat, and the less **new fat** you create, the more **old fat** it can burn!

"Makes sense."

Luckily, if you decide you do want to change the way you eat, there are a lot of easy things you can do:

"Like...?"

Well: How do you feel about "wasting food?"

"Hate it!"

A crime, is it?

"—of the worst kind!"

How about: "cleaning your plate?"

"Makes me think of Mother Teresa."

That good, huh?

"Oh, definitely!"

Gives you kind of a warm glow, does it?

"All over!"

Good. And what kind of glow do you think it **would** give you if it weren't **total nonsense**?

"What?!"

You heard us!

"Get outta here!"

And not just **harmless** nonsense! Oh no: it's a good bet that more lives have been ruined around this little bit of nonsense than around any other nonsense in history.

"But everyone knows—"

You're right: "everyone knows." So nobody "questions." Except one person:

"Who?"

A Dr. Joyce Bockar.

"Who's that?"

She wrote a book a few years back: *The Last Best Diet Book*. Finally "blew the lid" off this "wasting food/cleaning your plate" insanity.

"Oh? How so?"

By proving that there **is** no such thing as wasting food and there **is** no "virtue" in cleaning your plate:

First of all: once you turn a cow into a hamburger, it can never again become a cow. So if anything was "wasted," it was "wasted" long before **you** got hold of it!

And no matter what you do — eat the burger or throw it away — you can't "unwaste" the cow. So why keep trying?

To **honor** the cow, perhaps? To thank her for giving up her life so you could have a Big Mac?

Well, nice thought, but better to "honor" a waistline that **can** be changed than a cow who can't!

"But what about all the people starving in China?"

What about them?

"Well, shouldn't you clean your plate because of them?"

Oh, absolutely!

"See?"

And after you clean one plate for the Chinese, when you're already stuffed, why not clean a second plate that you don't want or need for all the starving Ethiopians?!

"I could do that."

And while you're sitting there, "dying" from all that overeating, do us a favor:

"What?"

—Try to figure out what effect "'cleaning your plate' in Des Moines" could possibly have on **anyone** starving **anywhere**!

"Well-l-l..."

Take your time: you'll need all you've got!

Why we fall for this nonsense — have **always** fallen for it — is beyond me!

Do you think those starving Ethiopians or Chinese are all huddled around a Western Union office somewhere, waiting for news of how much food you're finishing in Iowa; and then jumping for joy when they hear you've finished it **all**?! Because that's the only benefit they're ever going to get from you "cleaning your plate!"

Forget it! Nobody anywhere cares how much you're eating, and "cleaning your plate" won't do any of them the slightest bit of good!

"Then why do parents keep pushing it?"

Because parents specialize in "guilt trips" and what they're saying is: if the kid in Ethiopia got hold of that much food, **he'd** finish it all, so why should you do any less?!

"Amazing!"

And what's the end result of all this "Einsteinian" logic?

Of course: you keep getting fatter and fatter and the kid in Ethiopia starves to death anyway. So show me the winner!

"OK. But aren't you forgetting one thing?"

What's that?

"—I paid good money for that food."

So?

"So, shouldn't I get my money's-**worth**?!"

Sure you should—

"I knew I'd 'get' you!"

—from everything else!

"Excuse me?"

Look, there's nothing wrong with "getting your money's-worth" from things that **enrich** your life — your house, your car, your computer, your camcorder, your dog.

But overeating doesn't enrich your life, it **destroys** it!

So the more you try to get your money's-worth out of **food**, the more **destruction** you cause! Which will **not** win you this year's Nobel Prize in Cleverness!

So stop doing it! Stop trying to get your money's-worth out of food, stop worrying about "wasting" it, stop claiming there's some "virtue" in cleaning your plate, stop—

"All right! Enough! I'll do it!"

No you won't.

"What do you mean?! I just told you I would!"

And I'm telling you you won't!

"Why won't I?"

Because you're "too far gone" — all of us are. We've been so brainwashed into believing that "cleaning your plate" and "not wasting food" are the most wonderful things we can do, that we're helpless to stop doing them!

"Oooh — that's bad!"

No: that's good!

"That's 'good?!'"

Of course:

Look, you can't get where you're going if you don't know where you're at! And now that we know where you're at — that you're always going to be "cleaning your plate," no matter what — getting where you're going becomes simple:

Just put a minimum amount of food on that plate!

If that's not enough to satisfy you, you can always go back for a minimally-loaded second plate, and a third, and a fourth, and on and on until, I guess, you pass out.

By starting out with a **minimum** quantity, you at least give yourself a **chance** to get full on a small amount, a **chance** to avoid packing in totally unnecessary calories.

The other way — loading your plate to the "max" — it doesn't matter if you do get full halfway through: you're going to finish that mountain of mush come Hell or high water, and regardless how much pain it leaves you in!

Why?

Because it's the right thing to do!

Fine! Do it! Don't fight it! All we're saying is: Just finish a teensy-weensy plateful, instead of half the food in Fontana! If that doesn't satisfy you, have another teensy-weensy plateful, then another. Like the ad says: "Don't worry: we'll make more!"

Another thing:

If you're like most abusive eaters, the nerve endings in your stomach that are supposed to signal "fullness" to your brain have been so battered and beaten by your abusive eating that they no longer do their job very well. As a result, you could be getting physically full after the first **third** of your "food mountain," and yet have **no way of knowing it** till you're almost finished, by which time it's too late.

So, in addition to doing what we've already suggested — taking your original "mountain" and dividing it up into, say, three or four little "hills" — we would ask you to do one more thing: take a reasonable **break** between each of those "hills!"

Why?

To give your battered nerves the extra time they need, to do what they were designed to do.

Again, if you're still hungry, there's always more food to be had. But at least give yourself the **chance** to be satisfied with less!

At first, of course, you'll resent the fact that this new way of portioning out food is making it impossible for you to eat as much as you always have. After all, food is your "love," your "buddy," and who likes to lose a "buddy?"

Well, all we can say is: let the one, minimum plateful be "buddy" enough, if that's all your body needs! Push anything more on that body and you enter into the realm of, "With friends like that...."

Our job is to get you thin; a lifetime program of exercise walking will do just that, regardless what you eat (within limits, obviously).

So don't for a minute think that we're **demanding** that you change the way you eat. We offer the above only because it reveals something about most of us — an inability to "waste food," etc. — that, once known, can be easily dealt with — **if one chooses**!

And if you can't deal with it or don't want to? No problem: just keep walking!

2) The second way to avoid overeating is the easiest:

Stay away from "all-you-can-eat" restaurants.

Since you always want to get your money's-worth, and since all-you-can-eat places are nothing more than bottomless pits, you'll never feel you've gotten your money's-worth on less than 10 or 20 pounds of food!

Again: that attitude is never going to change, so avoid all-you-can-eat places like the Plague!

3) Another simple trick for changing your eating habits is to just delay your first feeding of the day for as long as you can.

Remember: the cravings you have for certain amounts or certain types of food are just an invention of the Subconscious Mind to get you doing the same things day after day; they rarely have anything to do with a **real** need for food.

So what?

So, you won't be killing yourself if you ignore them every once in a while.

And what will that do?

Well, in the same way you "train" your Subconscious to make you hungry for an omelet at 7:30 tomorrow by having one at 7:30 today, you can "train" your Subconscious to make you **not** hungry for an omelet at 7:30 tomorrow by **ignoring** the hunger you have for one at 7:30 today (which came about, most likely, because you had one at 7:30 yesterday!)

The Subconscious will, of course, try again at 8 o'clock, then 8:30, then 9:00, etc., since it thinks you really do need that omelet to survive and it wouldn't be doing its job if it didn't keep making you hungry for one.

And eventually, of course, you **will** give in to its demands because eventually you'll **have** to, to keep your energy up — which is the only reason food exists.

All we're saying is: try to give in to your Subconscious as **late** as possible, not as **early**, because nearly all of its demands will be false ones, and every false demand you can ignore on Day One will be one fewer demand you will have to contend with on Day Two.

Why?

Because every false demand you live through will show your Subconscious that you **don't** need to overeat every half hour to get from one day to the next (skinny people certainly don't), and it will stop trying to make you do so!

In other words, you will make "not eating" as much of a habit as "eating" ever was, and any time you can make something a habit, so that doing it becomes automatic, your race is all but won.

"But what about 'breakfast?'"
What about it?
"Well, if I keep eating later and later, I'll miss it!"
So?
"Well, it's only the most important meal of the **day**, you know!"
Is it?
"Of course it is! Everybody knows that!"
Do they?
"Sure!"
How?
"Well, they just do, that's all!"
Come on — you know how: **advertising**!

Let me ask you: who would you want coming to work for you in the morning: someone whose blood is chock full of nutrients from the previous night's meal and is now totally available for brain work, or someone whose blood supply is "trapped" in his stomach — far, far from that wonderful brain — trying to digest all manner of hotcakes and sausage and muffins and butter and cheese and God-knows-what-else?

Thank you!

So how did breakfast come to be the "most important meal of the day?" Well, if **you** owned shares in General Mills, or Aunt Jemima, or Jimmy Dean's, how "important" would **you** want breakfast to be?!

That's what we thought!

Not that there's anything wrong in helping a corporation pay its bills! It's just that, in the case of food, which is "lethal" to an eater like you, you might stop and ask yourself if all that eating is satisfying a real need or just a need that Daddy BigBucks has created for you, to help his profit-and-loss statement!

In the case of breakfast, sad to say, it's a "created" need.

How do we know?

Well, just go without breakfast for a few days and see how much **more** alert you are, how much **more** energy you have in the morning, all else being equal!

Of course, if you do find your energy "flagging" during the morning — if you've used up all your previous day's food — then by all means have something to eat! But at least give your body a **chance** to use all of yesterday's food before you dump any **more** food on it just because **someone else** told you to!

Look, it's really simple:

> The more you eat, the more you
> > want to eat,
> > need to eat,
> > can eat;

> The less you eat, the less you
> > want to eat,
> > need to eat,
> > can eat.

These are basic laws; they can't be broken:

You get along on less by "training" your body to get along on less — not by stuffing yourself! The more you have today, the **more** you'll want tomorrow; the less you have today, the **less** you'll want tomorrow.

As we've said, the Subconscious Mind takes notes on what you eat each day. If you survive to the next day, it assumes you did so **because** of what you ate. So it gets you to eat, the next day, exactly what you ate the day before, thinking that's what you need to do, to survive.

That pattern is never going to change. You can either use the knowledge to your advantage and start ignoring some of these false demands, or you can keep giving in to them, believing you're "really hungry" for hotcakes-and-bacon at 7:30, a couple of donuts at 9:00, a fudge brownie at 10:00, a double cheeseburger-and-fries at 11:30, a tuna sandwich at 2:00, a bag of peanuts at 3:00, a candy bar at 4:00, etc., and that, if you didn't satisfy these "real hungers," you'd starve to death!

Either way, it makes no difference to us.

Our job here is to get you thin and keep you thin, and that you can do without ever skipping a meal.

It's just that when you know why you eat the way you do, you at least have a chance to do something about it.

Of course, if you don't want to, you don't have to.

All you "**have**" to do is Thinwalk every day and you can kiss your obesity good-bye forever!

It's just that, if you **can** change your eating habits a little bit, you can kiss it good-bye that much sooner!

And isn't there someone you know who'd get a kick out of **that**?!

36
"Breakfast"

In the last chapter, we said that the only reason breakfast exists is to make breakfast companies rich; that whatever energy you need in the morning can be supplied by the previous day's food, but that these guys (cereal companies, egg companies, dairy companies, etc.) have brainwashed us into believing otherwise.

We weren't, we hate to say, being totally fair:

When you sit in a typical coffee shop and watch fat people smother their pancakes ("Large stack, please!") or French toast ("'Texas-size,' if you've got it!) with all manner of butter, syrup, jelly, sugar, etc., you soon realize that these addicts need no help at all!

If anything, you almost think that they're the ones who've come up with this "most important meal of the day" nonsense, simply to justify gorging themselves one more time, but without feeling guilty about it (after all, how bad could you be if you're doing nothing less than feeding yourself the "most important meal of the day?!")

True to their nature, instead of finding ways to do **without** those extra calories, fat people have once again found a way to **validate** them, since without them, the "poor souls" would be forever on the brink of starvation!

Before you make your daily "buy" into that myth, you might want to stop and ask yourself the real reason you're stuffing your face at 7 or 8 or 9 in the morning. Are you really "staving off starvation," or is there something else going on here?

We don't care, one way or the other, since, as long as you Thinwalk for an hour a day, you will cancel out all those calories. It's just that it's not a bad idea to try to eliminate all the calories you don't really need. That way, if you happen to **miss** a Thinwalking session, those calories won't enter your system "unopposed!"

So try to take a little more active role in what you put into your mouth. Try to avoid blindly stuffing your face, imagining that if you aren't **conscious** of what you're putting there, it won't make its way to your waistline!

That's a "fool's game," and we know you're no fool!

37
"No Sweat!"

There's a "craze" that rears its silly-but-dangerous head from time to time and that you should be on the lookout for: people trying to convince you that you can **sweat** yourself thin!

Those who push this insanity count on you knowing two things:

    1) people who exercise sweat, and
    2) people who exercise get thin.

What they then try to make you believe is that it's the **sweating** that's getting the exercisers thin — not the **exercise**!

So their job becomes simple: just get you to sweat like Niagara every time you so much as **think** about moving a muscle!

Which they do — with airtight plastic suits, pore-sealing skin creams, sweat clothes, etc.

No problem there, except that by doing one thing — artificially increasing the amount you sweat — they're actually **keeping** you from doing the other: losing weight!

"What?"

Absolutely:

The only "weight" worth losing is "fat;" whatever weight you lose in the form of water has to be replenished right after exercising or the only exercise you'll soon be doing deals strictly with daisies!

The only way you lose fat is by burning calories: the more

calories you burn, the more fat you lose; the fewer calories you burn, the less fat you lose. Laws of Nature.

So, anything that **stops** calorie-burning actually **stops** weight loss.

And how do you **stop** calorie burning?
Well, what are calories burned for?:

1) To maintain an internal temperature of 98.6° F. (37° C.)
Obviously, any time you **help** the body maintain that temperature, by holding heat in with airtight clothing, excess clothing, etc., you relieve the body of the need to burn **calories** to do so.

So, the more heat you hold in, the fewer calories your **body** has to burn to keep you warm and the less fat you lose.

2) To provide energy for our muscles.
Muscles are designed to work best—and burn the most calories — at some "optimum" temperature (that same "98.6° F."); raise that temperature and they won't burn as many calories.

How do you raise their temperature? By holding heat **in** instead of letting it escape.

Again: the more heat you hold in, the more heat accumulates around the muscles, the fewer calories they can burn and the less fat you lose.

So the "bottom line" is: the **more** you sweat artificially, by holding heat in, the **fewer** calories your body will **have** to burn and **can** burn, and the **less** real weight you'll lose!

"Are you saying I should run around naked when it's 20 below?!"
No: we want **thin** people, not **dead** ones!

What I'm saying is that you should wear just enough clothing to be "comfortable" at the start of your run — not too hot, not too cold. As long as you're "comfortable" at the start, then the amount you sweat will be the "right" amount, the "natural" amount.

In other words: all your sweat will be due to "calories being burned" ("good sweat") and not "heat unable to escape" ("bad sweat"). And the **amount** you sweat will be an accurate indication of how much weight you're **losing** — rather than how much weight you're **preventing** yourself from losing!

So always dress in a way where you expose as much of your skin as possible to the air, but not at the risk of freezing to death!

And always remember: the **less** you sweat, for a given amount of exercise, the **more** real weight you'll lose!
Hard to believe — but absolutely true!

38
"Why, Indeed?"

Earlier, we told you why we wanted you to get thin: to increase the overall happiness of the world.
We'd like to expand on that a bit:

The main reason to get thin is:

There is nothing you can do, fat, that you can't do better, thin. Nothing!

The Thin You will look better, feel better, move better, relate better that the Fat You ever could; the Thin You will get jobs, promotions, friends that the Fat You never could.

In short: you should get thin because life is so much **easier** for thin people!
You want a challenge? Take up bridge, or chess, or try to make some sense out of rugby. But don't keep challenging the world to accept you and love you as a fat person because it's never going to happen — no matter how many "fat-acceptance" groups spring up and no matter how many of them you join.
The world is not set up to love fat people. The obvious reason is that body fat is repulsive to most people's eyes. But there's more to it than "cosmetics:"

Someone who is noticeably overweight has at least one more psychological problem than someone who isn't. Nothing wrong with that, except that "well" people don't want to be around "sick" people — psychological or otherwise. Not because they think the sickness will rub off on them, but because they know that, when the chips are down, such people are more likely to give in to their natural instincts and go running off into a corner somewhere with their cookies and milk, rather than digging in and toughing it out!

They will never **voice** that concern — we humans are too nice to hurt someone else's feelings — but it will be the underlying reason why the fat person is never given jobs that he otherwise deserves, promotions that he's otherwise earned, friendships that would be automatic if he were thin, etc.

Oh sure: there are a lot of fat people out there you could trust with your life. But which ones are they? I can't tell. Can you?!

So it's easier for the thin world to simply "play the percentages," dismiss all fat people as "unreliable" and never run the risk of getting "burned" by one!

A "bum rap?" Perhaps. But it's the way of the world and it's never going to change.

If you want to have a better-than-even chance of being accepted, respected, loved, hired, promoted, etc., you're going to have to be thin. Every pound of overweight puts you that much further from any or all of those things.

But what, you might ask, will getting thin do?

"After all, I'll be the same person. If I was unworthy of all those things, fat, I'll be just as unworthy, thin!"

The answer, of course, is that you **won't** be the same person:

When you get thin, you bring none of your former physical life with you. People see you and respond to what they see — even those who have known only a Fat You their whole lives.

They begin treating you the way they treat every other thin person: with confidence that you can do the job, since they have no physical indication that you can't.

So what happens? Of course: You **do the job**!

You always had the ability; it's just that no one wanted to take a chance on you. When they do, you respond in kind.

The main thing they give you, though, is what they give all their thin friends: the opportunity to fail! Without that, you have virtually no chance to succeed, because there is no such thing as success without a backdrop of failure.

So when you fail, as you must, they let you try again. And again. And still again, until you succeed — a courtesy they never accord fat people!

Why do they do this? Because you are thin and thin people **always** succeed, so why should you be any different?!

You get the point: in the same way that "the job makes the man," so it is with being thin: being thin makes people **treat** you thin, which makes you **act** thin.

And all it takes is to **get** thin!

All we're asking is that you give the Thin World a try. With the Walk Yourself Thin program, it's so easy and pleasant to do we can't see any reason for not doing it!

And if, after being thin for a while, you decide that you preferred the way the world was treating you, fat? No problem: just return to your fatness.

But now that there is a simple way to eliminate excess bodysize, at least give thinness a try! All you need to do is act responsibly for one hour a day.

Of course, if you **can't** do that, maybe the world has been right about you all along!

39
If You Smoke

If you smoke, you shouldn't.

Of course, if you've figured out which end of the cigarette to light, you already know that.

However, if you not only smoke but are overweight as well, then you're **really** tempting fate and you might want to try **something** to reduce that "double jeopardy!"

Since smoking is such a hard habit to "kick" (harder than heroin, according to most), let's forget that one for a moment and work on the other one: your weight problem.

Like everyone else, the solution to that problem is easy: exercise.

Which exercise?

Well, what would you say about an exercise that not only got you thin in the shortest time possible, but would **let you smoke while you were doing it** (save your breath: as former smokers ourselves, we already know the answer!)?

Naturally, you most likely won't be able to walk as fast or as far as someone your size and age who doesn't smoke. But that's OK: you're only walking to get thin — not set the land speed record — and who cares how long it takes to happen as long as it happens, and happens without making you give up one of your most favorite things?

So go out there and enjoy those cigarettes (no one ever smoked because he **didn't** enjoy it; that's not what drugs are all about) every Thinwalking step of the way!

If some day you can give up smoking, all the better. But if you can't, no problem: at least Thinwalking will have given you a fighting chance to do **something** about outliving your parents or grandparents!

40

"It's a Boy!"

One of life's great joys is: having children.

For the figure-conscious woman, one of life's great miseries can be: having children!

The trick?: to have the "joy" without the "misery."

The trick?: Thinwalk.

There are obviously two ways of keeping your figure during pregnancy: eat less or exercise more.

If anybody out there thinks that eating less during pregnancy is a smashing idea, please leave your name with the parole officer!

I guess if you're a board-certified nutritionist, you can point to your food and state with certainty that "this can go" but "this must stay." Me? I wouldn't take a chance: give the little guy everything you can and let **him** "tell" you what he doesn't want!

Which only leaves "exercising more," if you want to stay as slim as possible during pregnancy and return to slimness as soon as possible thereafter.

We already know that in the long run, Thinwalking wins out over every other exercise. But it can be an even bigger hit in the short run: specifically, the short run known as "pregnancy."

The reason for this is that you would like to do an exercise almost up to the time of delivery, without feeling like you're "delivering" every time you do the exercise (those of you who've tried aerobic dancing in your eighth month know what I'm talking about!)

If ever there was a less jarring way than Thinwalking to safely burn bushels of calories without harming the baby, I'm not aware of it. In fact, I sometimes think that Thinwalking is God's gift to pregnant women, and that all the rest of us are just borrowing it for a little while.

And its value is more than just "cosmetic:"

It is a known fact that **fit** women have easier deliveries, all else being equal, than **non**-fit women. So not only does Thinwalking help you look better without hurting the baby, it also makes it easier to bring that baby into the world.

So if you want to stay as slim as possible during your pregnancy without depriving your baby of any nutrients, want to help your delivery, and want to get back into shape as quickly as possible after the baby is born, you have only one choice — and it's not: "pink?" or "blue?"

41

"It's that Time of Month..."

My wife's period started this morning; we had no warning. So what?

Well, normally by this time, we're in divorce court, dividing up our assets (a 24-year-old car; three cats [one pregnant]; and what's left of a set of K Mart's finest china!)

Why the difference this month?
She resumed her exercise program (in her case: running.)
Is it really that significant?
Well, when she's **not** running, she goes through monthly changes even **Freud** couldn't figure out! Catatonics run from her!
Yet this month: nothing!

So I asked her about it.
"Oh sure: Nothing stops PMS better than exercise — not 'hormones,' not Oil of Evening Primrose, nothing!"
For you or for everybody?
"'Everybody,' unless all the papers are lying!"

She handed me some of those papers and they seemed to bear her out:
All things considered, exercising women suffer far fewer and far less severe symptoms of PMS than their "couch potato-ette" cousins!

Will **you**? We don't know. But neither will you unless you get off that couch and start Thinwalking.

If the exercise has no effect on your PMS, nothing lost (except maybe a few dress sizes!); if it does, you may "save" more than a monthly clothing bill (your marriage, for one!)

If you want to read more on the subject, check out your local library. You might even try walking there!

42
The Kiddie Korps

Is there a sadder sight than "Fat children of fat parents?"

The best thing about a new day is that it gives us a fresh start, another chance to do it right! The same holds true for every new generation.

So every time we see a new generation making the exact same mistakes as the one before it, we get a very sick, very hopeless feeling in the pit of our stomach.

How miserable adults could want the same misery for their children is incomprehensible. And yet, there they are: little kids who are obese copies of their obese mommies and daddies, and who will have the same problems — physical and social — as their "porky" parents.

(It puts us in mind of the father, during the Vietnam War, who said: "If **I** could go and get shot at for my country [in World War II], then my **son** can very well get shot at for his country!" As if "getting shot at for your country" was some kind of great thing every generation should do, whether or not there was any **reason** for doing it!

(When we heard this father, we were kind of hoping he'd say: "I got shot at for my country so my son would never **have** to!" But he didn't.)

What's the solution to this generation-after-generation of fatness?

Well, you can't take the child out of the home. And you can't undo 5 or10 years of upbringing that has "told" the child: "Abusive eating is just fine! Your daddy and I do it, don't we?!")

So it would be a waste of time to get the child to stop doing what his mommy and daddy are saying is "Quite all right" to do.

Which leaves only "exercise," if we're going to get the child thin.

But which exercise?

Fortunately, that's an easy question to answer:

If you think fat **parents** are reluctant to move, take a gander at fat **children** some time! Talk about "glaciers!"

So anyone who is thinking of prescribing a program of vigorous exercise for these kids is not someone we want on our team in the next Mental Olympics!

What else?

What else: Thinwalking!

I mean, what kid could object to a strenuous **stroll** now and then?!

How hard could it be to put one foot in front of the other for an hour a day — especially when doing so will very likely offset all the calories that nobody has the heart to deny him?!

And is it really the worst thing we can do for our kids, making them responsible for their own actions ("If you eat now, you're gonna have to walk later!")?

We may be way off base with this, but it seems to us that the happiest kids are those whose parents **aren't** picking up after them all the time; who **aren't** driving them "two blocks here," "three blocks there," etc.

We know it's tough **not** to give the kids all the things we didn't have but thought we wanted — like "maid service." But, if those things do nothing to improve the child, is it really in his/her best interests to get them?!

Just a thought.

It's common knowledge that, no matter how much is wrong with a child, he will get most of his problems sorted out by the age of 40. All we're saying here is: why not get at least **one** of those problems sorted out by the age of 12, or 15, and save him or her those extra few decades of heartbreak?

And if you overweight kids out there are reading this, you know what "heartbreak" I'm talking about!

So why not take what is the easiest, most pleasant way out of your jam, and start walking yourself thin right now?!

You'll thank yourself — and love yourself — for doing it!

43
When You're Thin

With all other weight-loss programs, it's: "If you get thin..." With Thinwalking, it's: "When you get thin..."

Since your thinness is inevitable, you can start working out, ahead of time, what your thin life will consist of.

The first thing you must do is come up with a set of clever rejoinders for all the compliments you will be receiving on your new shape (if you **don't** come up with these responses, you'll soon start boring yourself to death with the same old lines.)

A few that we like are:

"It went off the way it went on: one ounce at a time! No one said much when it went on, but we're sure happy to hear how you feel now that it's off!"

"You noticed?!" (this is especially favored by people who have taken off, like, two or three hundred pounds!)

"I just wish I had started sooner!"

"...and I **feel** a whole lot better, too!"

"I'd **love** to have lunch with you!"

And so on.

The next thing you'll tackle is your wardrobe. Specifically:

you'll start adding one color you didn't dare buy when you were fat — and it ain't "black!"

You'll also have to re-map your walking routes, to take in all the full-length windows you so studiously avoided when you were fat.

Don't worry: You won't admire yourself for more than five or ten minutes in each one, so there's almost no chance of your children starving to death before you get back, unless, of course, they haven't eaten yet this month.

Should you feel guilty, spending so much time admiring yourself? Not at all! Why else did you get thin?!

Another thing we hope you'll want to do is devote more time to your fellow Thinwalking Club members, helping them to the same feelings you're now experiencing.

Remember: all else being equal, thin people are happier than fat people, so the thinner you make others, the happier you make yourself!

Which brings us to the "bottom line:" above all else, plan to **enjoy** your new life. I defy anyone to prove that we were put on this planet for any reason other than to enjoy it (just because so many **don't** or **can't** doesn't change the issue!)

And, in a private moment, be quietly grateful that you were lucky enough and courageous enough to pull yourself out of a hole that had no bottom; that you've given yourself a life you can look forward to living each day; that you've walked yourself thin!

44
One Last Word

So this is what the rest of your life will look like:

1) You will Thinwalk every day, going as fast as you comfortably can for as long as you comfortably can.

2) You will walk for any reason you want to, except one: to get thin!

3) You will make no drastic changes in your eating habits — unless you feel you can, without jeopardizing your Thinwalking.

4) You will never weigh yourself.

5) You will lose one or two ounces of bodysize each day (a bit more if you add "reduced eating" to your Thinwalking) until the **inevitable day** that you are down to your ideal body size.

6) You will never see any changes in your physique, nor will you expect to, from the start of your Thinwalking Program till the day you achieve your optimum body size.

7) You will keep a record of your progress, if that suits you, but you will never be a "slave" to it.

8) When you are ready — physically and/or psychologically — you will try every other exercise your heart desires.

9) You will dress in a way that **minimizes** sweating, so you can **maximize** "calorie burn."

10) If you do decide to go on a "diet," sometime during your Thinwalking program, you will promise yourself that, if the most-likely-ineffective "diet" makes you so weak that it threatens your

guaranteed-effective Thinwalking, you will abandon that "diet" immediately and return to just walking yourself thin.

You will find that the beauty of Thinwalking — and the feature that makes it so completely different from all other slimming programs (especially "diets") — is that it **builds on itself**:

The more you do, the more you **can** do;
The more bodysize you lose, the more bodysize you **can** lose and **do** lose.

And only one thing is required: that you begin!

And once you do begin, we see no reason why you won't quickly join the ranks of other Thinwalkers, who have made the greatest discovery of all about Thinwalking:

The more you do it, the more you **want** to do it.

A little bit like — well, that's another book!

For now, just get out and

Walk Yourself Thin!

—and make the whole **World** a lot happier place to live!

45
The Log

What follows is a Daily Log for charting your Thinwalking progress.

You must "keep" this log!

If you don't, we will find out and you will be severely thrashed!

We've made it as simple for you as we could (lots of check marks instead of essay questions!) We would, however, ask you to be as complete as you can in the sections requiring your comments.

If you don't want to write in this book — if, for example, you don't own it — just photocopy a two-page "set" of Log pages as many times as you need to and create your own Log book.

As you will notice, our main concern is with "subjective" impressions ("you" being the "subject"): how you feel, overall; how your legs feel; how easy your walk was; etc.
Though we've also allocated space for "objective" results — things evaluated by some "object" (like a "stopwatch" or a "yardstick") — we consider those far less important than finding out how **you** are changing from day to day (which is why most of these

"objective" measurements are placed at the bottom of the page and are labeled "Optional").

After you finish your initial 14-day Log, we would like to see it. Just photocopy the completed Log and send it to us at Moon River Publishing.

And if you have any suggestions for **improving** the Log, for God's sake don't keep them to yourself! We will pay handsomely (two, three dollars maybe) for all good suggestions.

Anyway, have fun with the Log and enjoy what it's telling you as you Walk Yourself Thin!

Daily Log

Day No.:_____ Date:_____ Approx. Time of Day:_____to _____

About how far did you walk today? _____

How does that distance compare with how far you walked yesterday?
- ☐ Much farther
- ☐ A little farther
- ☐ About the same
- ☐ Not as far

About how fast did you walk today (on average?)
- ☐ Over 30 min./mile
- ☐ 25-30 min./mile
- ☐ 20-25 min./mile
- ☐ 17-19 min./mile
- ☐ 15-16 min./mile
- ☐ 13-14 min./mile
- ☐ 10-12 min./mile
- ☐ Less than 10

How does this compare with how fast you walked yesterday?
- ☐ Much faster
- ☐ A little faster
- ☐ About the same
- ☐ A little slower

How did your leg muscles feel at the start of your walk?
- ☐ Loose and "fluid"
- ☐ About "normal"
- ☐ Somewhat "stiff"
- ☐ Very "stiff"
- ☐ Painful
- ☐ "Tired" or "Empty"

How did your leg muscles feel at the mid-point of your walk?
- ☐ Loose and "fluid"
- ☐ About "normal"
- ☐ Somewhat "stiff"
- ☐ Very "stiff"
- ☐ Painful
- ☐ "Tired" or "Empty"

How did your leg muscles feel at the end of the walk?
- ☐ Loose and "fluid"
- ☐ About "normal"
- ☐ Somewhat "stiff"
- ☐ Very "stiff"
- ☐ Painful
- ☐ "Tired" or "Empty"

How would you describe the way you were breathing at the "height" of your walk?
- ☐ With great difficulty
- ☐ With some difficulty
- ☐ "Normally"
- ☐ Very easily

What clothing size were you able to fit into this morning?
- ☐ Slack size:
- ☐ Dress size (if applicable):

How would you describe the "fit?"
- ☐ Very tight
- ☐ Somewhat tight
- ☐ "Just right"
- ☐ A bit loose
- ☐ Very loose
- ☐ Walked right out of them!

Overall Impressions and Comments on Your Progress:

Optional Walking Log:

Lap Length:_____

Lap No.	1	2	3	4	5	6	7	8
Lap Time								
Cum. Time								

Comments:

Daily Log

Day No.:_____   Date:_____   Approx. Time of Day:_____to _____

About how far did you walk today? _____

How does that distance compare with how far you walked yesterday?
- ☐ Much farther   ☐ About the same
- ☐ A little farther   ☐ Not as far

About how fast did you walk today (on average?)
- ☐ Over 30 min./mile   ☐ 20-25 min./mile   ☐ 15-16 min./mile   ☐ 10-12 min./mile
- ☐ 25-30 min./mile   ☐ 17-19 min./mile   ☐ 13-14 min./mile   ☐ Less than 10

How does this compare with how fast you walked yesterday?
- ☐ Much faster   ☐ About the same
- ☐ A little faster   ☐ A little slower

How did your leg muscles feel at the start of your walk?
- ☐ Loose and "fluid"   ☐ Somewhat "stiff"   ☐ Painful
- ☐ About "normal"   ☐ Very "stiff"   ☐ "Tired" or "Empty"

How did your leg muscles feel at the mid-point of your walk?
- ☐ Loose and "fluid"   ☐ Somewhat "stiff"   ☐ Painful
- ☐ About "normal"   ☐ Very "stiff"   ☐ "Tired" or "Empty"

How did your leg muscles feel at the end of the walk?
- ☐ Loose and "fluid"   ☐ Somewhat "stiff"   ☐ Painful
- ☐ About "normal"   ☐ Very "stiff"   ☐ "Tired" or "Empty"

How would you describe the way you were breathing at the "height" of your walk?
- ☐ With great difficulty   ☐ "Normally"
- ☐ With some difficulty   ☐ Very easily

What clothing size were you able to fit into this morning?
- ☐ Slack size:
- ☐ Dress size (if applicable):

How would you describe the "fit?"
- ☐ Very tight   ☐ "Just right"   ☐ Very loose
- ☐ Somewhat tight   ☐ A bit loose   ☐ Walked right out of them!

Overall Impressions and Comments on Your Progress:

Optional Walking Log:
Lap Length:_____

Lap No.	1	2	3	4	5	6	7	8
Lap Time								
Cum. Time								

Comments:

Daily Log

Day No.:_____ Date:_____ Approx. Time of Day:_____to _____

About how far did you walk today? _____

How does that distance compare with how far you walked yesterday?
- ☐ Much farther
- ☐ A little farther
- ☐ About the same
- ☐ Not as far

About how fast did you walk today (on average?)
- ☐ Over 30 min./mile
- ☐ 25-30 min./mile
- ☐ 20-25 min./mile
- ☐ 17-19 min./mile
- ☐ 15-16 min./mile
- ☐ 13-14 min./mile
- ☐ 10-12 min./mile
- ☐ Less than 10

How does this compare with how fast you walked yesterday?
- ☐ Much faster
- ☐ A little faster
- ☐ About the same
- ☐ A little slower

How did your leg muscles feel at the start of your walk?
- ☐ Loose and "fluid"
- ☐ About "normal"
- ☐ Somewhat "stiff"
- ☐ Very "stiff"
- ☐ Painful
- ☐ "Tired" or "Empty"

How did your leg muscles feel at the mid-point of your walk?
- ☐ Loose and "fluid"
- ☐ About "normal"
- ☐ Somewhat "stiff"
- ☐ Very "stiff"
- ☐ Painful
- ☐ "Tired" or "Empty"

How did your leg muscles feel at the end of the walk?
- ☐ Loose and "fluid"
- ☐ About "normal"
- ☐ Somewhat "stiff"
- ☐ Very "stiff"
- ☐ Painful
- ☐ "Tired" or "Empty"

How would you describe the way you were breathing at the "height" of your walk?
- ☐ With great difficulty
- ☐ With some difficulty
- ☐ "Normally"
- ☐ Very easily

What clothing size were you able to fit into this morning?
- ☐ Slack size:
- ☐ Dress size (if applicable):

How would you describe the "fit?"
- ☐ Very tight
- ☐ Somewhat tight
- ☐ "Just right"
- ☐ A bit loose
- ☐ Very loose
- ☐ Walked right out of them!

Overall Impressions and Comments on Your Progress:

Optional Walking Log:
Lap Length:_____

Lap No.	1	2	3	4	5	6	7	8
Lap Time								
Cum. Time								

Comments:

Daily Log

Day No.:_____   Date:_____   Approx. Time of Day:_____to _____

About how far did you walk today? _____

How does that distance compare with how far you walked yesterday?
- ☐ Much farther
- ☐ A little farther
- ☐ About the same
- ☐ Not as far

About how fast did you walk today (on average?)
- ☐ Over 30 min./mile
- ☐ 25-30 min./mile
- ☐ 20-25 min./mile
- ☐ 17-19 min./mile
- ☐ 15-16 min./mile
- ☐ 13-14 min./mile
- ☐ 10-12 min./mile
- ☐ Less than 10

How does this compare with how fast you walked yesterday?
- ☐ Much faster
- ☐ A little faster
- ☐ About the same
- ☐ A little slower

How did your leg muscles feel at the start of your walk?
- ☐ Loose and "fluid"
- ☐ About "normal"
- ☐ Somewhat "stiff"
- ☐ Very "stiff"
- ☐ Painful
- ☐ "Tired" or "Empty"

How did your leg muscles feel at the mid-point of your walk?
- ☐ Loose and "fluid"
- ☐ About "normal"
- ☐ Somewhat "stiff"
- ☐ Very "stiff"
- ☐ Painful
- ☐ "Tired" or "Empty"

How did your leg muscles feel at the end of the walk?
- ☐ Loose and "fluid"
- ☐ About "normal"
- ☐ Somewhat "stiff"
- ☐ Very "stiff"
- ☐ Painful
- ☐ "Tired" or "Empty"

How would you describe the way you were breathing at the "height" of your walk?
- ☐ With great difficulty
- ☐ With some difficulty
- ☐ "Normally"
- ☐ Very easily

What clothing size were you able to fit into this morning?
- ☐ Slack size:
- ☐ Dress size (if applicable):

How would you describe the "fit?"
- ☐ Very tight
- ☐ Somewhat tight
- ☐ "Just right"
- ☐ A bit loose
- ☐ Very loose
- ☐ Walked right out of them!

Overall Impressions and Comments on Your Progress:

Optional Walking Log:
Lap Length:_____

Lap No.	1	2	3	4	5	6	7	8
Lap Time								
Cum. Time								

Comments:

Daily Log

Day No.:_____ Date:_____ Approx. Time of Day:_____to _____

About how far did you walk today? _____

How does that distance compare with how far you walked yesterday?
- ☐ Much farther   ☐ About the same
- ☐ A little farther   ☐ Not as far

About how fast did you walk today (on average?)
- ☐ Over 30 min./mile   ☐ 20-25 min./mile   ☐ 15-16 min./mile   ☐ 10-12 min./mile
- ☐ 25-30 min./mile   ☐ 17-19 min./mile   ☐ 13-14 min./mile   ☐ Less than 10

How does this compare with how fast you walked yesterday?
- ☐ Much faster   ☐ About the same
- ☐ A little faster   ☐ A little slower

How did your leg muscles feel at the start of your walk?
- ☐ Loose and "fluid"   ☐ Somewhat "stiff"   ☐ Painful
- ☐ About "normal"   ☐ Very "stiff"   ☐ "Tired" or "Empty"

How did your leg muscles feel at the mid-point of your walk?
- ☐ Loose and "fluid"   ☐ Somewhat "stiff"   ☐ Painful
- ☐ About "normal"   ☐ Very "stiff"   ☐ "Tired" or "Empty"

How did your leg muscles feel at the end of the walk?
- ☐ Loose and "fluid"   ☐ Somewhat "stiff"   ☐ Painful
- ☐ About "normal"   ☐ Very "stiff"   ☐ "Tired" or "Empty"

How would you describe the way you were breathing at the "height" of your walk?
- ☐ With great difficulty   ☐ "Normally"
- ☐ With some difficulty   ☐ Very easily

What clothing size were you able to fit into this morning?
- ☐ Slack size:
- ☐ Dress size (if applicable):

How would you describe the "fit?"
- ☐ Very tight   ☐ "Just right"   ☐ Very loose
- ☐ Somewhat tight   ☐ A bit loose   ☐ Walked right out of them!

Overall Impressions and Comments on Your Progress:

Optional Walking Log:
Lap Length:_____

Lap No.	1	2	3	4	5	6	7	8
Lap Time								
Cum. Time								

Comments:

Daily Log

Day No.:_____ Date:_____ Approx. Time of Day:_____to _____

About how far did you walk today? _____

How does that distance compare with how far you walked yesterday?
     ☐ Much farther   ☐ About the same
     ☐ A little farther   ☐ Not as far

About how fast did you walk today (on average?)
   ☐ Over 30 min./mile   ☐ 20-25 min./mile   ☐ 15-16 min./mile   ☐ 10-12 min./mile
   ☐ 25-30 min./mile   ☐ 17-19 min./mile   ☐ 13-14 min./mile   ☐ Less than 10

How does this compare with how fast you walked yesterday?
     ☐ Much faster   ☐ About the same
     ☐ A little faster   ☐ A little slower

How did your leg muscles feel at the start of your walk?
     ☐ Loose and "fluid"   ☐ Somewhat "stiff"   ☐ Painful
     ☐ About "normal"   ☐ Very "stiff"   ☐ "Tired" or "Empty"

How did your leg muscles feel at the mid-point of your walk?
     ☐ Loose and "fluid"   ☐ Somewhat "stiff"   ☐ Painful
     ☐ About "normal"   ☐ Very "stiff"   ☐ "Tired" or "Empty"

How did your leg muscles feel at the end of the walk?
     ☐ Loose and "fluid"   ☐ Somewhat "stiff"   ☐ Painful
     ☐ About "normal"   ☐ Very "stiff"   ☐ "Tired" or "Empty"

How would you describe the way you were breathing at the "height" of your walk?
     ☐ With great difficulty   ☐ "Normally"
     ☐ With some difficulty   ☐ Very easily

What clothing size were you able to fit into this morning?
     ☐ Slack size:
     ☐ Dress size (if applicable):
How would you describe the "fit?"
     ☐ Very tight   ☐ "Just right"   ☐ Very loose
     ☐ Somewhat tight   ☐ A bit loose   ☐ Walked right out of them!

Overall Impressions and Comments on Your Progress:

Optional Walking Log:
Lap Length:_____

Lap No.	1	2	3	4	5	6	7	8
Lap Time								
Cum. Time								

Comments:

Daily Log

Day No.:_____ Date:_____ Approx. Time of Day:_____to _____

About how far did you walk today? _____

How does that distance compare with how far you walked yesterday?
- ☐ Much farther
- ☐ A little farther
- ☐ About the same
- ☐ Not as far

About how fast did you walk today (on average?)
- ☐ Over 30 min./mile
- ☐ 25-30 min./mile
- ☐ 20-25 min./mile
- ☐ 17-19 min./mile
- ☐ 15-16 min./mile
- ☐ 13-14 min./mile
- ☐ 10-12 min./mile
- ☐ Less than 10

How does this compare with how fast you walked yesterday?
- ☐ Much faster
- ☐ A little faster
- ☐ About the same
- ☐ A little slower

How did your leg muscles feel at the start of your walk?
- ☐ Loose and "fluid"
- ☐ About "normal"
- ☐ Somewhat "stiff"
- ☐ Very "stiff"
- ☐ Painful
- ☐ "Tired" or "Empty"

How did your leg muscles feel at the mid-point of your walk?
- ☐ Loose and "fluid"
- ☐ About "normal"
- ☐ Somewhat "stiff"
- ☐ Very "stiff"
- ☐ Painful
- ☐ "Tired" or "Empty"

How did your leg muscles feel at the end of the walk?
- ☐ Loose and "fluid"
- ☐ About "normal"
- ☐ Somewhat "stiff"
- ☐ Very "stiff"
- ☐ Painful
- ☐ "Tired" or "Empty"

How would you describe the way you were breathing at the "height" of your walk?
- ☐ With great difficulty
- ☐ With some difficulty
- ☐ "Normally"
- ☐ Very easily

What clothing size were you able to fit into this morning?
- ☐ Slack size:
- ☐ Dress size (if applicable):

How would you describe the "fit?"
- ☐ Very tight
- ☐ Somewhat tight
- ☐ "Just right"
- ☐ A bit loose
- ☐ Very loose
- ☐ Walked right out of them!

Overall Impressions and Comments on Your Progress:

Optional Walking Log:
Lap Length:_____

Lap No.	1	2	3	4	5	6	7	8
Lap Time								
Cum. Time								

Comments:

Daily Log

Day No.:_____ Date:_____ Approx. Time of Day:_____to _____

About how far did you walk today? _____

How does that distance compare with how far you walked yesterday?
- ☐ Much farther
- ☐ A little farther
- ☐ About the same
- ☐ Not as far

About how fast did you walk today (on average?)
- ☐ Over 30 min./mile
- ☐ 25-30 min./mile
- ☐ 20-25 min./mile
- ☐ 17-19 min./mile
- ☐ 15-16 min./mile
- ☐ 13-14 min./mile
- ☐ 10-12 min./mile
- ☐ Less than 10

How does this compare with how fast you walked yesterday?
- ☐ Much faster
- ☐ A little faster
- ☐ About the same
- ☐ A little slower

How did your leg muscles feel at the start of your walk?
- ☐ Loose and "fluid"
- ☐ About "normal"
- ☐ Somewhat "stiff"
- ☐ Very "stiff"
- ☐ Painful
- ☐ "Tired" or "Empty"

How did your leg muscles feel at the mid-point of your walk?
- ☐ Loose and "fluid"
- ☐ About "normal"
- ☐ Somewhat "stiff"
- ☐ Very "stiff"
- ☐ Painful
- ☐ "Tired" or "Empty"

How did your leg muscles feel at the end of the walk?
- ☐ Loose and "fluid"
- ☐ About "normal"
- ☐ Somewhat "stiff"
- ☐ Very "stiff"
- ☐ Painful
- ☐ "Tired" or "Empty"

How would you describe the way you were breathing at the "height" of your walk?
- ☐ With great difficulty
- ☐ With some difficulty
- ☐ "Normally"
- ☐ Very easily

What clothing size were you able to fit into this morning?
- ☐ Slack size:
- ☐ Dress size (if applicable):

How would you describe the "fit?"
- ☐ Very tight
- ☐ Somewhat tight
- ☐ "Just right"
- ☐ A bit loose
- ☐ Very loose
- ☐ Walked right out of them!

Overall Impressions and Comments on Your Progress:

Optional Walking Log:
Lap Length:_____

Lap No.	1	2	3	4	5	6	7	8
Lap Time								
Cum. Time								

Comments:

Daily Log

Day No.:_____ Date:_____ Approx. Time of Day:_____to _____

About how far did you walk today? _____

How does that distance compare with how far you walked yesterday?
- ☐ Much farther
- ☐ A little farther
- ☐ About the same
- ☐ Not as far

About how fast did you walk today (on average?)
- ☐ Over 30 min./mile
- ☐ 25-30 min./mile
- ☐ 20-25 min./mile
- ☐ 17-19 min./mile
- ☐ 15-16 min./mile
- ☐ 13-14 min./mile
- ☐ 10-12 min./mile
- ☐ Less than 10

How does this compare with how fast you walked yesterday?
- ☐ Much faster
- ☐ A little faster
- ☐ About the same
- ☐ A little slower

How did your leg muscles feel at the start of your walk?
- ☐ Loose and "fluid"
- ☐ About "normal"
- ☐ Somewhat "stiff"
- ☐ Very "stiff"
- ☐ Painful
- ☐ "Tired" or "Empty"

How did your leg muscles feel at the mid-point of your walk?
- ☐ Loose and "fluid"
- ☐ About "normal"
- ☐ Somewhat "stiff"
- ☐ Very "stiff"
- ☐ Painful
- ☐ "Tired" or "Empty"

How did your leg muscles feel at the end of the walk?
- ☐ Loose and "fluid"
- ☐ About "normal"
- ☐ Somewhat "stiff"
- ☐ Very "stiff"
- ☐ Painful
- ☐ "Tired" or "Empty"

How would you describe the way you were breathing at the "height" of your walk?
- ☐ With great difficulty
- ☐ With some difficulty
- ☐ "Normally"
- ☐ Very easily

What clothing size were you able to fit into this morning?
- ☐ Slack size:
- ☐ Dress size (if applicable):

How would you describe the "fit?"
- ☐ Very tight
- ☐ Somewhat tight
- ☐ "Just right"
- ☐ A bit loose
- ☐ Very loose
- ☐ Walked right out of them!

Overall Impressions and Comments on Your Progress:

Optional Walking Log:
Lap Length:_____

Lap No.	1	2	3	4	5	6	7	8
Lap Time								
Cum. Time								

Comments:

Daily Log

Day No.:_____   Date:_____   Approx. Time of Day:_____to _____

About how far did you walk today? _____

How does that distance compare with how far you walked yesterday?
- ☐ Much farther   ☐ About the same
- ☐ A little farther   ☐ Not as far

About how fast did you walk today (on average?)
- ☐ Over 30 min./mile   ☐ 20-25 min./mile   ☐ 15-16 min./mile   ☐ 10-12 min./mile
- ☐ 25-30 min./mile   ☐ 17-19 min./mile   ☐ 13-14 min./mile   ☐ Less than 10

How does this compare with how fast you walked yesterday?
- ☐ Much faster   ☐ About the same
- ☐ A little faster   ☐ A little slower

How did your leg muscles feel at the start of your walk?
- ☐ Loose and "fluid"   ☐ Somewhat "stiff"   ☐ Painful
- ☐ About "normal"   ☐ Very "stiff"   ☐ "Tired" or "Empty"

How did your leg muscles feel at the mid-point of your walk?
- ☐ Loose and "fluid"   ☐ Somewhat "stiff"   ☐ Painful
- ☐ About "normal"   ☐ Very "stiff"   ☐ "Tired" or "Empty"

How did your leg muscles feel at the end of the walk?
- ☐ Loose and "fluid"   ☐ Somewhat "stiff"   ☐ Painful
- ☐ About "normal"   ☐ Very "stiff"   ☐ "Tired" or "Empty"

How would you describe the way you were breathing at the "height" of your walk?
- ☐ With great difficulty   ☐ "Normally"
- ☐ With some difficulty   ☐ Very easily

What clothing size were you able to fit into this morning?
- ☐ Slack size:
- ☐ Dress size (if applicable):

How would you describe the "fit?"
- ☐ Very tight   ☐ "Just right"   ☐ Very loose
- ☐ Somewhat tight   ☐ A bit loose   ☐ Walked right out of them!

Overall Impressions and Comments on Your Progress:

Optional Walking Log:
Lap Length:_____

Lap No.	1	2	3	4	5	6	7	8
Lap Time								
Cum. Time								

Comments:

Daily Log

Day No.:_____   Date:_____   Approx. Time of Day:_____to _____

About how far did you walk today? _____

How does that distance compare with how far you walked yesterday?
- ☐ Much farther
- ☐ A little farther
- ☐ About the same
- ☐ Not as far

About how fast did you walk today (on average?)
- ☐ Over 30 min./mile
- ☐ 25-30 min./mile
- ☐ 20-25 min./mile
- ☐ 17-19 min./mile
- ☐ 15-16 min./mile
- ☐ 13-14 min./mile
- ☐ 10-12 min./mile
- ☐ Less than 10

How does this compare with how fast you walked yesterday?
- ☐ Much faster
- ☐ A little faster
- ☐ About the same
- ☐ A little slower

How did your leg muscles feel at the start of your walk?
- ☐ Loose and "fluid"
- ☐ About "normal"
- ☐ Somewhat "stiff"
- ☐ Very "stiff"
- ☐ Painful
- ☐ "Tired" or "Empty"

How did your leg muscles feel at the mid-point of your walk?
- ☐ Loose and "fluid"
- ☐ About "normal"
- ☐ Somewhat "stiff"
- ☐ Very "stiff"
- ☐ Painful
- ☐ "Tired" or "Empty"

How did your leg muscles feel at the end of the walk?
- ☐ Loose and "fluid"
- ☐ About "normal"
- ☐ Somewhat "stiff"
- ☐ Very "stiff"
- ☐ Painful
- ☐ "Tired" or "Empty"

How would you describe the way you were breathing at the "height" of your walk?
- ☐ With great difficulty
- ☐ With some difficulty
- ☐ "Normally"
- ☐ Very easily

What clothing size were you able to fit into this morning?
- ☐ Slack size:
- ☐ Dress size (if applicable):

How would you describe the "fit?"
- ☐ Very tight
- ☐ Somewhat tight
- ☐ "Just right"
- ☐ A bit loose
- ☐ Very loose
- ☐ Walked right out of them!

Overall Impressions and Comments on Your Progress:

Optional Walking Log:
Lap Length:_____

Lap No.	1	2	3	4	5	6	7	8
Lap Time								
Cum. Time								

Comments:

Daily Log

Day No.:_____   Date:_____   Approx. Time of Day:_____to _____

About how far did you walk today? _____

How does that distance compare with how far you walked yesterday?
- ☐ Much farther
- ☐ A little farther
- ☐ About the same
- ☐ Not as far

About how fast did you walk today (on average?)
- ☐ Over 30 min./mile
- ☐ 25-30 min./mile
- ☐ 20-25 min./mile
- ☐ 17-19 min./mile
- ☐ 15-16 min./mile
- ☐ 13-14 min./mile
- ☐ 10-12 min./mile
- ☐ Less than 10

How does this compare with how fast you walked yesterday?
- ☐ Much faster
- ☐ A little faster
- ☐ About the same
- ☐ A little slower

How did your leg muscles feel at the start of your walk?
- ☐ Loose and "fluid"
- ☐ About "normal"
- ☐ Somewhat "stiff"
- ☐ Very "stiff"
- ☐ Painful
- ☐ "Tired" or "Empty"

How did your leg muscles feel at the mid-point of your walk?
- ☐ Loose and "fluid"
- ☐ About "normal"
- ☐ Somewhat "stiff"
- ☐ Very "stiff"
- ☐ Painful
- ☐ "Tired" or "Empty"

How did your leg muscles feel at the end of the walk?
- ☐ Loose and "fluid"
- ☐ About "normal"
- ☐ Somewhat "stiff"
- ☐ Very "stiff"
- ☐ Painful
- ☐ "Tired" or "Empty"

How would you describe the way you were breathing at the "height" of your walk?
- ☐ With great difficulty
- ☐ With some difficulty
- ☐ "Normally"
- ☐ Very easily

What clothing size were you able to fit into this morning?
- ☐ Slack size:
- ☐ Dress size (if applicable):

How would you describe the "fit?"
- ☐ Very tight
- ☐ Somewhat tight
- ☐ "Just right"
- ☐ A bit loose
- ☐ Very loose
- ☐ Walked right out of them!

Overall Impressions and Comments on Your Progress:

Optional Walking Log:
Lap Length:_____

Lap No.	1	2	3	4	5	6	7	8
Lap Time								
Cum. Time								

Comments:

Daily Log

Day No.:_____   Date:_____   Approx. Time of Day:_____to _____

About how far did you walk today? _____

How does that distance compare with how far you walked yesterday?
- ☐ Much farther
- ☐ A little farther
- ☐ About the same
- ☐ Not as far

About how fast did you walk today (on average?)
- ☐ Over 30 min./mile
- ☐ 25-30 min./mile
- ☐ 20-25 min./mile
- ☐ 17-19 min./mile
- ☐ 15-16 min./mile
- ☐ 13-14 min./mile
- ☐ 10-12 min./mile
- ☐ Less than 10

How does this compare with how fast you walked yesterday?
- ☐ Much faster
- ☐ A little faster
- ☐ About the same
- ☐ A little slower

How did your leg muscles feel at the start of your walk?
- ☐ Loose and "fluid"
- ☐ About "normal"
- ☐ Somewhat "stiff"
- ☐ Very "stiff"
- ☐ Painful
- ☐ "Tired" or "Empty"

How did your leg muscles feel at the mid-point of your walk?
- ☐ Loose and "fluid"
- ☐ About "normal"
- ☐ Somewhat "stiff"
- ☐ Very "stiff"
- ☐ Painful
- ☐ "Tired" or "Empty"

How did your leg muscles feel at the end of the walk?
- ☐ Loose and "fluid"
- ☐ About "normal"
- ☐ Somewhat "stiff"
- ☐ Very "stiff"
- ☐ Painful
- ☐ "Tired" or "Empty"

How would you describe the way you were breathing at the "height" of your walk?
- ☐ With great difficulty
- ☐ With some difficulty
- ☐ "Normally"
- ☐ Very easily

What clothing size were you able to fit into this morning?
- ☐ Slack size:
- ☐ Dress size (if applicable):

How would you describe the "fit?"
- ☐ Very tight
- ☐ Somewhat tight
- ☐ "Just right"
- ☐ A bit loose
- ☐ Very loose
- ☐ Walked right out of them!

Overall Impressions and Comments on Your Progress:

Optional Walking Log:
Lap Length:_____

Lap No.	1	2	3	4	5	6	7	8
Lap Time								
Cum. Time								

Comments:

Daily Log

Day No.:_____ Date:_____ Approx. Time of Day:_____to _____

About how far did you walk today? _____

How does that distance compare with how far you walked yesterday?
☐ Much farther   ☐ About the same
☐ A little farther   ☐ Not as far

About how fast did you walk today (on average?)
☐ Over 30 min./mile   ☐ 20-25 min./mile   ☐ 15-16 min./mile   ☐ 10-12 min./mile
☐ 25-30 min./mile   ☐ 17-19 min./mile   ☐ 13-14 min./mile   ☐ Less than 10

How does this compare with how fast you walked yesterday?
☐ Much faster   ☐ About the same
☐ A little faster   ☐ A little slower

How did your leg muscles feel at the start of your walk?
☐ Loose and "fluid"   ☐ Somewhat "stiff"   ☐ Painful
☐ About "normal"   ☐ Very "stiff"   ☐ "Tired" or "Empty"

How did your leg muscles feel at the mid-point of your walk?
☐ Loose and "fluid"   ☐ Somewhat "stiff"   ☐ Painful
☐ About "normal"   ☐ Very "stiff"   ☐ "Tired" or "Empty"

How did your leg muscles feel at the end of the walk?
☐ Loose and "fluid"   ☐ Somewhat "stiff"   ☐ Painful
☐ About "normal"   ☐ Very "stiff"   ☐ "Tired" or "Empty"

How would you describe the way you were breathing at the "height" of your walk?
☐ With great difficulty   ☐ "Normally"
☐ With some difficulty   ☐ Very easily

What clothing size were you able to fit into this morning?
☐ Slack size:
☐ Dress size (if applicable):
How would you describe the "fit?"
☐ Very tight   ☐ "Just right"   ☐ Very loose
☐ Somewhat tight   ☐ A bit loose   ☐ Walked right out of them!

Overall Impressions and Comments on Your Progress:

Optional Walking Log:
Lap Length:_____

Lap No.	1	2	3	4	5	6	7	8
Lap Time								
Cum. Time								

Comments:

Appendix A

A New Term

When you go on a "diet," you lose weight, which is measured in "pounds."

When you walk yourself thin, on the other hand, you might **not** lose any weight; you might only lose **size**, which you **can't** measure in "pounds."

However, every pound of **weight** ("fat") takes up a certain amount of **space** (has a certain size), so if you lost that amount of **size** it would be as if you'd lost that amount of **weight** (fat), no matter how much **actual** weight you'd lost.

For a variety of reasons, it would be nice to have some way to equate the amount of **size** you lose by Thinwalking with the amount of **weight** you would have lost if you'd dieted yourself down to that same size. In fact, there is such a way, through a term we call a "**size-pound**," which is nothing more than

the amount of space that a pound of fat takes up.

Since, with Thinwalking, all we care about is losing "space" ("size"), all we're interested in is "size-pounds:" how many you still are; how many you've lost; how many you still need to lose; etc.

When you go on a "diet," you say: "I have to lose 40 pounds." With Thinwalking, you say: "I have to lose 40 size-pounds," which is the amount of size you would lose if you lost 40 pounds of fat, regardless how much weight you'll **actually** be losing.

To use myself as an example:

If I "diet" myself down to 160 pounds, from a starting weight of 200, I can fit into Size 32 slacks; I would have lost 40 size-pounds, which, as it happens, is the same number of "actual" pounds I lost, since I did it all through dieting.

However, if I walk myself thin from the same starting point, I can get into those Size 32 slacks at a scale weight of 175, because I didn't just **lose** the fat, I "converted" a lot of it into muscle, which is **not weightless**.

In the second case, even though I've lost only 25 "actual" pounds, I would still have lost the same 40 "size-pounds." In other words, I will have gotten down to the same **size** as I would have if I had simply lost 40 **pounds**!

Since body size is all I care about, "size-pounds" are the only things that matter.

In other words: I wouldn't care if I **gained** 50 "actual" pounds by walking; as long as I lost 40 **size**-pounds and could fit into those Size 32 slacks, the program would have done its job!

So don't worry about "actual" pounds. Just worry about losing bodysize — measured, if necessary, in "size-pounds" — and you'll be "home free!"

Index

A

A-list 51
abusive eaters 85, 93
accomplishment 71
"ache-y" 13
achievements 70
active role 3, 62
"actual" pounds 135, 136
ad 93
addictive 4, 57
addicts 98
"adjusted" 8
admiration 63
adult 63, 87, 88, 112
advertising 95
aerobic dancing 109
airtight clothing 101
alcoholics 54
"alive & kicking" 5
"all ears" 19
"All-you-can-eat" restaurants 94
alley 85
America 1, 76
anger 7
angles 26, 79
animal starch 15
anthems 14
"anti-survival" 41
anxiety 50, 52
Arbuckle, Fatty 39

arms 26, 30
Army tents 77
assets 110
assumption 16
athletes 14
attitudes 81, 94
Aunt Jemima 96
awards 4

B

baby 50, 108, 109
"baby" 87
bad feelings 63
bad information 64
bad sweat 102
bathroom scale 38, 60
"bathwater" 87
battered nerves 93
Beautiful New You 4
beer 56
beer companies 4
being fat 7, 64, 67, 77
being thin 78, 105
benefit 82, 91
"best exercise" 10, 11
best friend 1, 74

"best life possible" 67
Big Macs 78. 90
bike 10
bikers 11
biking 9, 10
bills 96
"biology" 17
black (color) 116
Black Lagoon 54
blindfold 23, 24
blizzards 10
blood 95, 96
blood flow 40
blood vessels 75
blubber 60, 79
"blue" 109
blur 70
boat 10
Bockar, Dr. Joyce 90
body 4, 5, 13, 15, 16, 17, 19, 26, 29, 30, 32,
  35, 37, 39, 40, 43, 44, 45, 46, 47, 48, 56,
  59, 60, 61, 62, 75, 79, 81, 83, 87, 93, 96,
  97, 101
body cells 46
body fat 35, 36, 42
body fluids 35
body of water 10
body size 6, 23, 26, 28, 34, 35, 75, 79, 117,
  136
bodysize 6, 30, 31, 32, 43, 64, 76, 105,
  117, 118, 136
bones 35
boozer 54
boss 51
"bottom line" 116
"bottomless pits" 94
bowel movement (delayed) 36
brain 8, 46, 93, 96
"break" 93
breakfast 54, 95, 96, 98
breakfast companies 98
bridge (card game) 103
broken muscles 16, 40
brushing teeth 25
"buddy" 93
buffalo 59, 60

buffaloville 60
"bum rap" 104
bumper sticker 8, 74
"bus" 31
bust shots 26
butt 72
butter 9, 40, 96, 98
"buy" 98

C

Ca-ca County 51
calculator 43
calorie(s) 5, 6, 10, 11, 12, 13, 36, 40,
  41, 42, 43, 45, 46, 47, 59, 60, 61,
  62, 92, 98, 99, 100, 101, 109, 113
calorie-burning 40, 101, 117
calorie count 49
calves 30
camcorder 92
candy 9
candy bars 51, 97
candy companies 98
car 54, 91, 110
catatonics 110
cats 110
cave 59
celebration 37
centuries 37
cereal companies 98
"chafing at the bit" 11
chair 7
challenge 16, 103
change of heart 86
charts 22, 74
chest 29, 30
cheese 96
"cheese!" 26
chess 1-3
children 47, 108, 112, 113, 116
china 110
China 90
Chinese 90
Christmas 79, 80
"chunkers" 3

cigarettes 81, 106, 107
circuit 20
"cleaning your plate" 89, 90, 91, 92
closet 80
clothes 1, 8, 26, 34, 77, 79, 80, 84
clothing 101
clothing bill, monthly 111
clothing sizes 20, 37
coffee 8
coffee shop 98
cold truth 55
comfort 65
companions 21
compliments 115
computer 59, 92
conflict 63
"confusion" 37
"Conservation Overdrive" 60
control 9, 39, 68, 69
cookie(s) 3, 4, 9, 40, 43, 49, 51, 52, 53, 74
cookie binge 49
cookie companies 78
cookie jar 4
cookie crumbs 69
cookies-and-milk 104
corporation 96
"cosmetics" 103, 109
cottage-cheese-and-tomato-slices 49
couch 13, 111
"couch potato" 34, 35
"couch potato-ette" 110
courtesy 105
courtrooms 4
cow 90
cravings 55, 94
"craze" 100
"created" need 96
creative thought 46
Creator 4, 76
creatures of habit 54
crib 51
"crime" 89
cross-country skiing 11
"curiosity killed the cat" 20
customers 47
cutback 46

D

Daddy 63 113
   obese, 112
Daddy Big Bucks 96
Daily Log 119
daily routine 25, 76
dairy companies 98
daisies 100
David 44
Day One 13, 16, 61, 83, 95
Day Twenty-one 16
Day Two 61, 95
"death-warmed-over" (face) 75
decade 10, 88
defense 86
degenerate slob 81
dehydrated soup 88
delivery 109
depression 7, 18
Des Moines 91
destiny 67
destruction 92
diaper rash 50
diet 45
"diet" 1, 5, 6, 35, 36, 39, 40, 41, 45, 47, 48, 49, 52, 57, 60, 61, 62, 75, 81, 85, 86, 87, 117, 118, 135, 136
"Diet Heaven" 85
"diet yourself thin" 68, 75
"Dieter's Hell" 60, 85
"dieting" 35, 41, 48, 59, 61, 62, 75, 136
dinner 54
disappointment 22, 24, 80
distance runners 15
distances 13, 21, 22, 83
Divorce Court 60, 110
doctor 3, 4
dog 92
donuts 55, 56, 97
doses 4, 71
"double bonus" 75
double cheeseburger 97
"double jeopardy" 67
"double 'overkill'" 16

"down a quart" 23
dreams 84
drinkers 54
drinking 68
driver 54
drugs 107

E

"earnest suggestions" 66
eating 25, 42, 57, 68, 76, 95
eating binge 18
eating cycle 57
eating habit(s) 56, 95, 97, 117
"eating hours" 69
egg companies 98
Einstein, Albert 31
"Einsteinian logic" 91
"Einstein's Corollary" 32
emergencies 17, 45
employer 47
"energized" 11
energy 15, 40, 41, 46, 59, 95, 96, 98, 101
environment 78
"essay questions" 74
Ethiopia 45, 49, 91
Ethiopians 90, 91
"every day is Christmas" 80
evil 66
evolution 47, 60
"exchange" 61
exercise 4, 9, 10, 11, 12, 17, 35, 36, 39,
    40, 41, 42, 45, 61, 68, 69, 70, 75, 76,
    77, 87, 100, 106, 108, 109, 110, 111,
    113, 117
exercise program 5, 35, 36, 76, 110
"exercise pushers" 4
exercise walking 94
exercised body 39
exercised muscles 61
"exercised" thin people 74
exercising women 110
expectations 28
"experts" 40
extra fuel 16

extra miles 16
extra speed 16
extra strength 16

F

face-on 26
failed families 7
failed opportunities 7
failed relationships 7
failure 105
false demands 56, 95, 97
false hungers 56
false readings 36
family 47
family doctor 3
famine 45
Fargo 9
fasting programs 86
fat 1, 4, 5, 6, 7, 8, 12, 16, 17, 24, 29, 30,
    32, 35, 40, 45, 46, 47, 52, 59, 60, 61,
    62, 70, 76, 77, 78, 81, 83, 85, 86, 87,
    89, 100, 101, 103, 104, 105, 116,
    135, 136
fat-burning 6, 12
fat-acceptance groups 103
fat calories 12
fat children 112, 113
fat loss 36
fat pad 16, 62, 63
fat parents 112, 113
fat people 4, 7, 40, 74, 76, 82, 83, 98,
    103, 104, 105, 116
fat person 67, 77
fat-pulling sequence 30
fat stores 29, 59, 62, 75
Fat You 103, 104
fate 106
"fatness" 105, 113
"fatties" 77
fault 4
feelings 104, 116
figure 108
figure-conscious woman f108
file clerk 7

fill-up 8
"fire below" 56
"fireworks" 55
fishing 8
fit 53, 70, 75
fit women 109
"five feet of fudge" 50
"5:30 drinkers" 54
flags 14
"flip side" 70, 77
floor 7
fluid 35, 36
Fontana 93
food 9, 36, 37, 50, 51, 52, 53, 57, 82, 91, 92, 93, 94, 95, 96, 98, 108
"food mountain" 93
food treat 37
fool 99
"fool's game" 99
football halfback 34
"forbidden fruit" 37
foundation 66
14-day Log 120
friends 81, 93, 103
friendships 104
French fries 9, 78, 97
French toast 98
Freud, Sigmund 110
front door 10
fudge 50
fudge brownie 97
full-body shots 26
"full cup" 8
"fullness" 93
future 3

G

garbage 36
gazelle 84
General Mills 96
generation 112, 113
genius 56
Georgia 49
get-thin program 11, 36, 37, 70

getting thin 8, 14, 19, 24, 63, 64, 67, 77, 78, 82, 84, 86, 104
glacier 3, 113
glorious face 75
glow 89
glycogen 15, 16, 61, 83
"glycogen burn" 61
goal(s) 18, 24, 39, 67, 70, 72
God's gift 109
Godsend 62
goldfish 34
Goliath 44
"gonzo" eating 9
good feelings 63
good sweat 102
gorgeous 6, 17, 24
grandparents 107
grapefruit-and-cottage cheese 38, 52
grave 68
"great equalizer" 44
great...great grandfather 59
"guaranteed ounce" 88
"guilt trips" 91
gut contents 35
gut "longing" 55

H

habit 54, 56, 57, 58, 70, 76, 95, 106
"half-a-grapefruit-and-black-coffee" 39
hamburger 90
"handle" 50
hands 60
happy 7, 8, 53, 70
happiness 8, 77, 103
"hare" 10
harm 56
Harvard 7
hatchet 87
head 30
headline 86
"healing" legs 84

"health" 4, 66, 74, 75
health builders 75
health risk 3
heart 24, 30, 46, 75, 113, 117
heart muscle 29
heart palpitations 55
heartbreak 114
heat 102
height 34
helplessness 50
heroin 106
Higher Level (of functioning) 46
"hills" (of food) 93
hips 82
history 90
"hitting the 'wall'" 15
hold-back 46, 47
hole 116
honor 90
hormones 24, 110
horror stories 40
hot fudge sundae 37, 51
hotcakes 96
hotcakes-and-bacon 97
hour 83, 87
"housekeeping" calories 42
humans 86
human companionship 57
hunger 50, 56
hunting grounds 59
hurricanes 10

I

ice cream cone 60
ideal body size 28
ill-at-ease 64
inch 18, 86
inches 1
"inches-per-week" 32
"infant" 87
infantile 69, 85
injuries 10
"insanity" 66, 100
insurance company 74

invention 94
investment 66
Iowa 91

J

"jackpot" 78
jail 51
jelly 98
jelly donut 55, 56
Jimmy Dean 96
job interviews 7
"job makes the man, the" 105
"job well done" 66
jobs 103, 104
joggers 10, 11
jogging 9
joy 2, 19, 27, 62, 71, 78, 91, 108
junior high school 81

K

K Mart 110
Kiddie Korps 112
kids 24, 112, 113
kiester 53
"killers" 35, 36
kitten 60

L

La-la Land 50, 51
land speed record 106
lap 20, 21
lap times 20, 21
Last Best Diet Book 90
laws 97
lawyers 3
leg(s) 13, 15, 17, 40, 62, 119
leg condition 21
leg muscles 6, 15, 29, 79
Lewis, Carl 39
library 111

life   2, 7, 12, 19, 25, 53, 55, 60, 63, 66,
     75, 78, 88, 90, 91, 92, 103, 104, 108,
     116, 117
"life-and-death proposition"   56
life insurance   86
life span   49
lifestyle   3
limits   94
lion   39
liquor companies   4
listless   13
little cars   8
lobotomy   28
long-distance runner   81
loop   20, 21
loophole   53
losing weight   5, 6, 36, 100
losses   135
lottery   87
love   27, 37, 61, 63, 79, 93
lover   51
Lower Level (of functioning)   45
"lumpy"   32
lunch   54, 81, 115
lung(s)   24, 46, 75
lung capacity   21

M

MBA   7
"machinery"   56
magazines   26
magic   59, 61, 62, 85, 86, 87, 88
maid service   113
"making the grade"   44
manager   8
marathon-and-a-half   42
"mark"   11
marriage   111
medals   14
mental attitude   19
mental survival   49
Mental Olympics   113
message   7
"metabolic furnaces"   62

"middle years"   84
mile(s)   16, 38, 40, 41, 83
mileage   18, 20, 21
millenium   13
"millimeters-per-month"   32
mind   1, 24, 37, 39, 57, 58, 60
miracle   15, 69, 71
miracle "diet"   60, 86, 87
mirror   27, 29, 31, 49, 84
misery   66, 108, 112
models   26
molecules   15
Mommy   50, 51, 63, 64
obese,   112
money   91
money's-worth   91, 92, 94
Moon   7
mountain of mush   93
"mountains of misery"   8
"mother lode"   69
Mother Teresa   89
mother's purse   81
mothers   81
mouth   99
"move around"   4
muffins   9, 96
Murphy   32
"Murphy" storehouses   32
Murphy's Law   30
Murphy's Law of Bodysize Loss
     30, 32
muscle(s)   6, 13, 15, 16, 17, 35, 40,
     44, 46, 61, 62, 82, 83, 84, 100,
     101, 136
muscle fibers   40, 83, 84
muscle rebuilding   16
muscle tissue   12
myth   98

N

"nails"   39
national debt   49
Nature   30, 60, 68, 88, 101
neck   30

need 56
neighborhood 21, 72
nerve endings 93
"nest" 51
New Age 62
new fat 89
new life 116
"new little cars" 8
new muscle 6
"new shape" 115
New You 24
newly-thin people 64
Niagara 100
Nobel Prize (Cleverness) 92
noble 47
non-alcoholics 55
non-exercised body 39
non-fat calories 12
non-fit women 109
non-magical self 87
non-"Murphy" storehouses 32
nonsense 89, 90, 91, 98
"normal" life 66
"not-eating" 95
"not wasting food" 92
notes 97
nutrients 95, 109
nutritionist, board-certified 108

O

obese 65, 112
obese people 64
obesity 2, 97
objective measurements 120
obsession 21
"ocean" (of calories) 60
odds-on choice 40
"off to the races" 60
oil of evening primrose 110
old fat 89
Olympics 22
omelets 9, 94, 95
"one-fell-swoop" school 86

"one-for-one" exchange 61
one-in-a-million 4
"one-inch-at-a-time" school 86
opportunity to fail 105
optimal life 67
Oreo cookie 40
organs 35, 75
ounces-per-day 23
"overdoing it" 13
overeating 91, 92, 94, 95
"overkill" 16
overnight 23, 52, 64
overweight 43, 50, 52, 81, 82,
    86, 88,
    104
overweight kids 114
oxygen tent 4

P

PMS 110, 111
pace 18
Pacific Ocean 23
pancakes 98
"papaya-and-pork rinds" 49
"papayas-and-prune juice" 88
paper 11
pain 93
parents 63, 91, 107, 113
park 21, 71
parole officer 108
pattern (eating) 97
"peak" 13
peanuts 97
performance 21
performance charts 19, 22
period (menstrual) 110
phone call 54
photo developer 26
photos 26
physical exercise 76
physical "fireworks" 55
physical shape 19
"physical" self 79

physical survival 49
physique 65, 81, 117
pictures 26, 27, 31
pin 7, 23, 24
"pink" 109
"pipedream pound" 88
pizza 9
Plague, the 94
"plant life" 70
plants 59
plastic suits 100
plow 34
pocketbook 78
"poor souls" 98
pore-sealing creams 100
poses 26
pounds 135, 136
"pounds-per-day" losses 41
power 61
"power molecules" 15, 40
prayers 69, 82
"precious" 50
predictability 65, 66
pregnancy 108, 109
pregnant women 109
pressure 29
primary goals 29
"pro-survival" 41
profit-and-loss picture 96
program 3, 22
progress 18, 19, 20, 21, 22, 26, 80, 117
progress chart 21
"progressoholic" 20
promotions 103, 104
protein 16
psychoanalysis 87
psychological problem 104
psychological reasons 57
psychologically "mature" 63
psychologists 50

Q

quarter-mile track 21

R

rabbit 86
racehorse 34
raw materials 16
"real hunger" 97
real-world slimming 23
rear 26
"recharge batteries" 17
record time 30
reduced eating 79, 117
reducing program 36
redwood tree 86, 87
reflection 38
report card 81
research 51
respect 63
river 20, 21
road 13
Rocky Mountains 21
rolls 9
"rolls" 4
round-trip ticket 60
rowers 11
rowing 10
rowing machine 10
rugby 103
run 40
running 10, 110
running track 1, 21
rut 83

S

"S. C." 49
sabotage 63
salad 69
salad bar 8, 49, 78
salad dressings 78
salt 35, 36
sandpaper 48
Sara Lee 4
sausage 96
scale 35, 37, 38, 85

"screwball" program 88
Scrooge 60
"seal of approval" 3
security 66
self-control 68
"selling" 4
"sending forth" 61
senses 23
sequence (fat-pulling) 30
session(s) 10, 12, 13, 22, 38, 84, 99
"seventh tear" 44
"sheer delight" 41
"shelf" 11
shares 96
Sherman, General Wm. T. 49
"shining moment" 70
shoe(s) 10, 54, 60
shopping 25
Shorter, Frank 82
shortfall 5, 46
shoulders 24, 30
side effect 29, 62
size 6, 8, 16, 34, 35, 135, 136
size-pound 28, 29, 83, 135, 136
skiers 10, 11
skiing 9, 10, 11
skin 81, 102
skinnier 6
skinny people 95
skis 10
slacks 31
slave 20, 117
sleeve 86
slim 4, 25, 30, 108
slimming 26
    programs 118
slimness 61, 108
smokers 54, 106
smoking 68, 106, 107
snacks 54
snapshot 27
"sneak preview" 47
Snickers Bars 51
snow 10
social reject 65

social rejection 52
solid food 88
"solution" (Subconscious) 52, 53, 57
sons 81
sore 13
soreness 13, 69
soul 40
space 135
Space Program 50
speed 12, 22, 83
speed record 18
spine 31
spirits 31, 71
sports watch 20, 21
"Stan" 81
starch 59
starvation 39, 46, 49, 50, 51, 55, 70, 87, 99
starvation diet 41
Starvation Patrol 51
steak 69
step test 60
stereo headphones 38
stomach 93, 96, 112
stomach-churning 55
stopwatch 119
storage 5, 16, 17, 45, 46, 87
stored fat 61
storehouses 30, 32
street 2, 71
strength 16
stroll 113
structures 31
Subconscious (Mind) 37, 48, 49, 50, 51, 52, 53, 55, 56, 57, 58, 59, 75, 94, 95, 97
success 105
sue-happy 3
sugar 98
sunburn 48
Sundays 72
surprises 4
survival 39, 45, 46, 47, 48, 49, 55, 56, 61
survival muscles 61

survival program 47
sweat 100, 101, 102
sweat clothes 100
swimmers 11
swimming 9, 10
syrup 98

T

tabloid 49
taking a shower 25
taking pictures 26
targets 18, 19
taxes 65
teacup (of fat) 60
"teeth" 39
temperature, internal 101
"10 K" 46
"tented" 4
term paper 51
terminal disappointment 36
territory 85
thighs 30, 32
"thimble time" 60
thimbleful (of blubber) 60
thin 1, 3, 4, 7, 8, 9, 10, 11, 12, 13, 14, 17, 19,
    22, 23, 24, 29, 30, 31, 37, 38, 39, 40, 41,
    42, 53, 56, 60, 62, 62, 64, 68, 69, 75, 82,
    86, 87, 88, 94, 97, 100, 103, 104, 105,
    106, 113, 115, 116
thin people 1, 4, 74, 77, 78, 101, 103, 105,
    116
Thin World 105
Thin You 103
thinness 24, 29, 77, 105, 115
Thinwalk 1, 11, 13, 15, 19, 44, 53, 56, 58,
    61, 66, 69, 70, 72, 83, 97, 99, 108, 117
Thinwalker 1, 19, 70, 118
Thinwalking 4, 5, 6, 11, 12, 13, 17, 18, 19,
    22, 23, 24, 25, 26, 28, 29, 30, 31, 32, 35,
    37, 38, 40, 41, 43, 44, 53, 56, 59, 61, 62,
    62, 64, 67, 69, 70, 71, 75, 76, 77, 78, 79,
    80, 82, 83, 84, 86, 87, 88, 89, 99, 107,
    108, 109, 111, 113, 115, 117, 118, 119,
    135

Thinwalking slimming 32
"Thinwalking Story" 17
threat (to survival) 39
three-tiered platforms 14
Thrival Level 46
thumb 23, 24
time 74
time-lapse camera 72
"times" 18, 19
tired 13
tobacco companies 4
today 55, 56, 57, 70, 73, 79, 94, 97
tomorrow 55, 56, 57, 73, 94, 97
tooth-and-nail 39
torment 47
"tortoise" 11
torture 9
total mileage 20, 21
track 2, 13, 71
"tree trunks" 82, 84
"trick" 94
trim 25
tuna sandwich 97
turn of the century 3
twice-thinking 47
"two-for-one" exchange 61

U

undernourished child 51
"unfat" 75
unhappiness 8, 77
"unmagical" results 87
Universal Truth 67

V

verdict 30
victim(s) 30, 38
Vietnam War 112
visible fat 17
vote 9

W

"wacko ward" 50

waistline 30, 31, 32, 43, 90, 99

walk 9, 12, 13, 14, 15, 16, 18, 20, 22, 24, 40, 42, 53, 56, 72, 117

walk yourself thin 3, 8, 11, 31, 47, 53, 61, 62, 75, 77, 82, 114, 116, 120, 135, 136

Walk Yourself Thin Program 1, 37, 79, 105

walking 4, 8, 10, 12, 15, 16, 18, 19, 21, 22, 31, 40, 43, 56, 94, 136

Walking Log 21

walking program 37, 56

walking routes 116

walking tour 1

"Wall," the 15

wardrobe 26, 32, 66, 86, 115

"wasting food" 89, 90, 94

watch 20, 82

water 85, 100

waterskiing 10

weak 87

weather 19

Week One 13

weight 6, 34, 35, 36, 37, 40, 41, 88, 100, 101, 102, 135, 136

weight gain 35, 45

weight loss 37, 46, 101

weight-loss pressure 29

weight-loss program 5, 35, 37, 66, 115

weight problem 106

weight-reduction program 87

Western Union office 91

whole-hearted try 78

windows 116

wine companies 4

"winner" 10, 91

Wonderful New You 86

working 8

workout 13, 46

world 1, 7, 27, 64, 66, 79, 103, 104, 105, 109, 118

world-class mileage 13

world-class speed 13

World War II 112

worldful (of calories) 60

worst enemy 1

XYZ

yardstick 119

year 10, 13, 14, 28, 29, 42, 43, 64, 88

yesterday 55, 57, 70, 95, 96

"zillion-calorie-a-spoonful" 78

zombie 47

Glossary

Abusive Eater: Someone who eats far in excess of what he needs to, to stay alive.

"Actual" Pounds: What a weighing scale tells you (see, for comparison, **Size-Pounds.**)

Addictive: The property of a substance that makes you want to consume it when you're not and makes it impossible to **stop** consuming it once you've started.

Adults: People able to exert some control over their own lives.

Aerobic Exercise: Exercise which uses the large muscles of the body long enough and hard enough that substantial quantities of oxygen (air) are required. Typical aerobic exercises: brisk walking; long-distance running; cycling; swimming; aerobic dancing.

All-you-can-eat Restaurants: "Bottomless pits," where you feel obligated to eat 20 or 30 pounds of food because they let you.

Anaerobic Exercise: Exercise done in short bursts, so that great quantities of oxygen (air) are not required for muscles to do their work. Examples: weightlifting; sprint races; tennis.

Animal Starch: See **Glycogen**.

Anti-Survival: Anything that hurts your chances of seeing tomorrow (see: **Starvation Diet**).

Anxiety: Feeling of helplessness that arises when you lose control of your life situation.

Arbuckle, Fatty: Silent-film comedian.

Bad Sweat: Sweat that comes from holding in body heat artificially (with airtight plastic suits, excess clothing, pore-sealing skin creams, etc.) Actually **reduces** the amount of real weight ("fat") that exercise is trying to burn off (see also: **Good Sweat**).

Bathroom Scale: Instrument invented in the Dark Ages to measure pain.

Best Life Possible: What everyone should try to live; may feature many things, but "being fat" isn't one of them.

Bockar, Dr. Joyce: Author of *The Last Best Diet Book*, which revealed "not wasting food" and the value of "cleaning your plate" to be the nonsense they truly are.

Body: Your constant companion.

Body Fat: Nature's reminder that excess calories don't always vanish from the Universe just because they vanish from sight!

Body Size: The size of your body.

Bodysize: The part of your body that you "lose" on the Walk Yourself Thin Program (known as "weight" on "diet" programs); measured in "size-pounds" (*which see*).

Bodysize-reduction Program: Method of reducing bodysize by exercise, which may or may not result in loss of weight (see: "**Walk Yourself Thin Program**").

Break-in Period: The first two weeks of Thinwalking, where the maximum number of muscle fibers are torn down, with new ones eventually built in their place; period of maximum soreness and muscle fatigue until new muscles get "on line."

Breakfast: Meal invented by food companies to increase their sales (see also: **Mother's Day; Father's Day; Secretary's Day;** etc.)

Burn-out (Muscle): Premature muscle "shutdown," due to trying too much too soon.

Bushelful: A unit of measure equal to four pecks.

Ca-ca County: Less-than-ideal place to live (see, for comparison: **La-la Land**).

Calorie: A unit of heat-energy that fuels everything we do: thought; muscle function; food processing; maintenance of body temperature; etc.; when "number ingested" exceeds "number used," the excess is stored as body fat (*which see*).

Catatonics: People who traditionally remain motionless for hours or days at a time.

Chafing at the Bit: What horses start doing when they're anxious to run.

Challenge: To "ask" more out of something than it normally delivers.

China: Most populous nation on Earth; main reason why millions of older Americans "clean their plate" at every meal (see also: **Ethiopia**).

Christmas morning: Traditionally, the most joyous morning of the year over most of the World.

Chunkers: Fat folk.

Cleaning your Plate: Considered by many to be the most virtuous thing a human being can do; impossible for abusive eaters **not** to do; cause of more human misery than all wars and diseases combined.

Clothing Sizes: The way Thinwalkers measure their progress.

Conservation Overdrive: The mechanism your body uses to **conserve** stored calories in the face of anything that threatens them ("starvation;" "'diets;'" etc.)

Control: Enforcing limits on your own or others' thoughts or actions.

Cosmetic: Referring to surface features only.

Couch: Piece of household furniture especially designed for growing certain types of potatoes (*which see*).

Couch Potato: Someone who spends vast amounts of time on a piece of household furniture, watching people who look the way he claims he wants to.

"Creature from the Black Lagoon:" Popular movie of the 1950's.

Cross-country Skiing: Terrific exercise that a lot of people talk about doing someday.

"Curiosity killed the Cat:"   Time-honored expression suggesting that some things are better left alone.

Cutback: Reduction in the number of calories you normally eat (see also: **Hold-back**).

Daddy Big Bucks: Corporate executive whose only job is to get you to spend as much money as possible (see also: **Breakfast**).

Daily Log: Method of charting your Thinwalking progress (see the one included with this book).

Daily Routine: Things you just do every day, without giving them a second thought (brushing your teeth; taking a shower; Thinwalking; etc.).

David: In the Bible: real short guy who specialized in killing real tall guys (see also: **Goliath**).

Des Moines: City in Iowa, supposedly typical of "middle America."

Diet: What you eat.

"Diet:"   A program that **changes** what you eat, in an effort to get you thin (see: **Temporary Fix**).

Double Bonus (from walking yourself thin): 1) Easier to do than "dieting;" 2) A healthier You when you get there.

Double Jeopardy: Refers to what a person places himself into when he not only is overweight, but smokes as well.

Double Overkill: When your body 1) restocks your muscles with more "power molecules" than your walk took out, and 2) builds stronger muscles than your walking tore down; the reason you can walk farther and faster on Day Fifty-one than you could on Day One.

Dream-world Slimming: Losing "pounds-per-day," day after day; i.e., something that can only happen in your dreams (see, for contrast: **Real-world Slimming**).

Eating binge: Cure for abusive eater's existing depression. Also: source of **next** depression.

Einstein, Albert: World-famous physicist who developed the Laws of Relativity.

Einstein's Corollary: "Everything is relative!" Applies to evaluating amount of bodysize an area has lost. Example: If lower chest has lost four inches, but waistline only one, waistline will actually appear to have gotten three inches **bigger** (see also: **Murphy's Law of Bodysize Loss**).

Endurance: Ability to continue a given activity for longer and longer periods of time.

Enemy: A non-friend: someone who is out to harm or hinder you. Refers here to what the Subconscious Mind seems to become when you try to "diet" yourself thin.

Ethiopia: Nation in East Africa known for mass starvations due to combination of long-term drought and civil war; main reason why millions of young Americans are told to "clean their plate" at every meal (see also: **China**).

Evolution: The horse we all rode in on.

Exercise: Method of getting thin by **using** calories rather than **restricting** them (see also: **"Diet"**).

Exercise Pushers: People who try to get you thin by having you do something **positive** — "exercise" — rather than something **negative**: "starvation."

Expectations: Birthplace of disappointment.

False Hunger: Physical feeling, generated by your Subconscious Mind, to satisfy its mental needs (psychological "survival").

Fargo: Pleasant town in North Dakota.

Fat: Our long-term reward for single-minded devotion to short-term pleasure ("overeating"); chemical that evolution has chosen for us to use, to store most of our excess energy.

Fat-Acceptance Groups: Collections of obese people who have banded together to convince the thin world and themselves that the things we've always known about fat people — inability to control their actions; repulsive appearance; general lack of personal responsibility; greater difficulty of movement; higher rate of absenteeism, due to chronic physical problems — are, in fact, all "lies!" In other words: that the entire population of Planet Earth has been "making these things up" for the last million years or so! Good luck!

Fat Pads: Biologically: stored energy; psychologically: stored misery!

File Clerk: Entry-level position in most companies, usually occupied by semi-skilled thin people or highly-skilled fat ones.

Fire Below: An intense longing in your gut for a particular substance (food; drug; etc.)

Fitness: Measure of your ability to meet life's challenges, both physical and mental.

Fontana: Small town in Southern California.

Food: The Subconscious Mind's "solution" to every abusive eater's problems.

Fool's Game: Imagining that something isn't happening just because you choose to ignore it.

Forbidden Fruit: Food whose consumption you can't honestly control and don't really want to.

Freud, Sigmund: Father of psychoanalysis (*which see*); Viennese neurologist who discovered infant sexuality.

Future: Something to look forward to or to dread, depending on what you do each day to shape it.

Gazelle: Fast-moving animal that bounds through forest and plain.

Getting Thin: Something done, a) with great difficulty, by crushing your mind and body in a vise ("starvation diet"), or b) with great ease, by putting one foot in front of the other for a year or two.

Glacier: The couch potato of rivers.

Glycogen: Also known as "animal starch;" stored in muscle and liver; made up of long strands of sugar molecules, strung together like beads in a necklace, which provide the quick energy needed for muscle movement, thought, etc.

Goal: The best way to bring order out of chaos.

Goliath: In the Bible: real tall guy who had a lot of trouble with real short guys (see also: **David**).

"Gonzo:" Anything done to excess.

Good Sweat: Sweat that results from "calories being burned" and not "heat being trapped;" encouraged by wearing the minimum amount of clothing while exercising (see, for contrast: **Bad Sweat**).

Grapefruit-and-cottage cheese: Terrific way to get permanently thin (see also: **Half-a-grapefruit-and-black coffee; Cottage cheese-and-tomato slices; Cruel joke; etc.**)

Guaranteed Ounce: Amount of daily bodysize loss that Thinwalking can offer (see, for contrast: **Pipedream Pound**).

Guilt trip: Highly-favored method to modify children's behavior.

Habit: Anything you do automatically, day after day.

Harvard: A prestigious university in Massachusetts.

"Have your cake and eat it, too:" Signifying "getting the best of both worlds" — usually, an impossibility.

Heartbreak: The sad feeling you get when things don't go the way you want them to go.

"Hitting the 'Wall:'" The point, during a walk or run, where your leg muscles have used up all available "quick-energy" molecules ("glycogen") and must turn to slow-burning fat or muscle tissue if you're going to keep moving.

Hold-back: Number of calories your body stops bringing out of storage for non-survival functions during periods of starvation (see also: **Cutback**).

Hormones: Chemicals that go whizzing around your body, solving problems (adrenaline) or causing them (PMS).

Housekeeping Calories: Energy used to rebuild muscles and restock them with "fuel" following exercise; often overlooked when evaluating effectiveness of exercise.

Infallible: What mommies and daddies are, until we're old enough to know better.

Infantile: Acting like an infant.

"Jackpot:" A corner you get painted into, from which there is no easy escape.

Kiester: Main contact point between couch potato and his vehicle of choice.

La-la Land: Where you go, to dream (see, for contrast: **Ca-ca County**).

Lap: Once around a walking "loop" (*which see*).

Laws of Eating: The more you eat, the more you
> want to eat,
> need to eat,
> can eat.

The less you eat, the less you
> want to eat,
> need to eat,
> can eat.

Lewis, Carl: World-champion sprinter.

Life-expectancy Chart: A reminder that there's more to being thin than just **looking** good!

Life-and-Death Proposition: What satisfying every single demand for food seems to be.

Lobotomy: A brain operation that increases one's appreciation of vegetables.

"Loop:" A "closed" (start/finish line the same) walking circuit (see also: **Lap**).

Loophole: Something you can slip through when nobody's looking.

Losing Weight: What you do temporarily on a "diet."

Losing Size: What you do permanently when you walk yourself thin.

Lottery: Game of chance which millions play but, statistically speaking, no one ever wins (see also: **Starvation Diet**).

Loving Others: Most important thing in life; impossible, if you don't love yourself (*which see*).

Loving Yourself: The whole point of the Walk Yourself Thin Program; prime prerequisite for loving others (*which see*).

MBA (Masters in Business Administration): A graduate-school degree that is a usual prerequisite for executive-level positions in a company.

Magic: When something happens that defies rational explanation; in other words, something that **can't** happen (see also: **Miracle**).

Maid Service: A great luxury, desired by all, whose main benefit is to earn money for the maid.

Marathon-and-a-half: Approximately 40 miles (marathon distance = 26.2 miles.)

Metabolic Furnaces: Exercised muscles, which give excess calories a chance to be burned rather than stored.

Millenium: One thousand years.

Miracle: Something that happens that defies rational explanation (see also: **Magic**).

Money's-worth: What you should get from things that **enrich** your life, not things that **destroy** it — like excess food.

Moon: Large chunk of rock that stays within a few hundred thousand miles of Earth for some reason.

Mother Lode: Literally: richest vein of precious-metal ore; figuratively: where the best results are to be found (see also: **Thinwalking**).

Mountains of Misery: Enormous barriers, keeping happiness from entering fat people's lives.

Mother Teresa: A saintly woman who works with the poor of India; winner of the Nobel Peace Prize.

"Murphy" Storehouses: Places where you would most like fat to leave, so it doesn't (see also: **Non-"Murphy" Storehouses**).

Murphy's Law (General):   If anything can go wrong, it will.

Murphy's Law of Getting Thin: Wherever you really want the bodysize to leave, that's where it won't.

Muscle: Protein-rich structure where the majority of calories that enter the body are burned (see also: **Metabolic Furnaces**).

National Debt: A number so high that no one can count to it.

New Day: God's gift to people in need of a "fresh start" (see also: **New Generation**).

New Generation: God's gift to civilizations in need of a "fresh start" (see also: **New Day**).

Niagara: Enormouse waterfalls at the U. S.-Canadian border in upstate New York.

Non-"Murphy" Storehouses: Places where you don't care if they get thin, so they do so right away (see also: **"Murphy" Storehouses**).

Obesity: Being fatter than you should be.

Obsession: Stronger-than-normal dedication to doing something.

Objective Measurements: Things measured with respect to some "object" — stopwatch, yardstick, etc. (see also: **Subjective Impressions**).

Oil of Evening Primrose: Holistic remedy for relief of premenstrual syndrome.

Odds-on Choice: Overwhelming favorite to do something.

On the Mark: Ready to exercise.

On the Shelf: Where over-exercisers usually wind up.

One-for-One Exchange: Where your body burns a calorie for every one your "diet" denies it (see also: **Two-for-One Exchange.**)

One-in-a-Million: The number of people who will get struck by lightning in their lifetime and/or who will be harmed by trying to walk themselves thin.

Overkill: More happening than you expected to happen.

Oxygen Tent: Plastic enclosure for providing higher-than-normal amounts of oxygen to critically-ill people.

"Papayas-and-Pork Rinds:" Nonsensical "diet" that millions of fat people will someday get around to trying (see also: **"Papayas-and-Prune Juice."**)

"Papayas-and-Prune Juice:" Alternate selection of the "'Diet' of the Month" Club.

Parole Officer: Someone responsible for the comings and goings of criminals.

Performance Charts: Records that people keep, to track the progress they're making; much beloved by obsessive-compulsives.

Photographs: Objects that "freeze" time; useful for measuring otherwise undetectable changes.

Physical Fireworks: Bodily changes (stomach-churning; gut longing; etc.) that make you crave certain things.

Pipedream Pound: Amt of daily weight loss that miracle "diets" promise (see, for contrast: **Guaranteed Ounce**).

Power Molecules: Biochemicals that give you quick energy (see: **Glycogen**).

Prayer: The only way you're going to get thin, if you refuse to lift a finger to help yourself.

Premenstrual Syndrome (PMS): The main reason divorce courts are doing so well.

Primary Goals (of Thinwalking): Beautifying leg muscles and stengthening heart muscle (see also: **Side Effect [of Thinwalking]**).

Pro-survival: Anything that increases your chances of seeing tomorrow (see also: **Exercise**; see, for contrast: **Anti-survival**).

Protein: Major ingredient of muscle tissue.

Psychoanalysis: Trying to figure out what ails you psychologically, by talking it out with a psychiatrist or psychoanalyst; developed by Sigmund Freud (*which see*).

Psychologists: People who try to figure out what's going on inside their own heads so they can tell you what's going on inside yours.

Real-world Slimming: Something which happens in ounces-per-day of bodysize (see, for contrast: **Dream-world Slimming**).

Rolls: Bakery products that get better with butter.

"Rolls:" Aftermarket body parts that **don't** get better with butter.

Rowing Machines: See: "The road to Hell is paved with good intentions."

Rugby: English game resembling American football, in which a lot is probably going on.

Running Track: To a Thinwalker: "Heaven-on-Earth;" To a couch potato: the thing that lets you know where the football field ends.

Sabotage: A conscious effort to destroy something.

Salad Bar: A place where you can get millions of calories-worth of "diet" foods.

Sara Lee: Manufacturer of the highest-quality commercial baked goods in history.

Scrooge, Ebenezer: Main character in Charles Dickens' "A Christmas Carol;" known for overall nastiness (see also: **Starvation Diet**).

Session: A relatively-prolonged time period, during which you do one thing almost exclusively.

"747:" Large aircraft that, ideally, goes higher and higher on take-off.

Seventh Tear: The point at which it becomes impossible to continue tearing paper.

Sherman, Gen. Wm. T.: Union General in the American Civil War (1861-65), who burned most of the state of Georgia while conquering it.

Shorter, Frank: Gold medalist in the Olympic marathon.

Shortfall: The difference between what you need or want and what you actually get.

Side Effect: The unavoidable consequence of trying to achieve a **primary** effect.

Side effect (of Thinwalking): Thinness (see also: **Primary Goals [of Thinwalking]**).

Size-pound: The amount of size a pound of body fat takes up.

Slave: Having your life under the control of someone or something else.

Social Rejection: Difficult for thin people to get; the birthright of fat folk.

Sore: An "ache-y" feeling in muscles, tendons, etc., due to those things being torn down but not yet rebuilt.

Sports Watches: Clever little timepieces that give you more information than IBM mainframes used to.

Starvation: Death due to lack of food; constant worry of overweight people, of no concern to normal-weight ones.

Starvation Diet: A time-honored way to take off 20 pounds and put back 30; also: ideal punishment for getting so fat.

Starvation Patrol: Group of people empowered to arrest mommies who don't feed their children every 20-30 seconds.

Staving off Starvation: What food addicts are doing with every 3,000-calorie meal.

Step Test: Method for evaluating heart function.

Store Windows: Best friends of newly-thin people.

Subconscious Mind: Portion of your brain designed to help you solve problems; receives strongest programming in infancy; therefore, "solutions" are often "infantile," and bear little relation to what would **really** solve the problem.

Subjective Impressions: How "you" — the "subject" — evaluate certain things (see also: **Objective Measurements**).

Survival Level (of Body Function): Calories used to keep heart beating, lungs breathing, kidneys filtering, etc. (see also: **Thrival Level**).

Tabloid: Newspaper, sold mainly in supermarkets, that tells us what we want to hear.

Targets: Performance goals.

"10 K:" Ten kilometers (= 6.21 miles.)

"The Man who Came to Dinner:" Story of a man who comes to dinner and never leaves (see also: **Waistline**).

Thin World, the: A place where people are treated a lot better than they were in the Fat World. Lone requirement for entry: being thin.

Thinwalk: What you go on, to walk yourself thin.

Thinwalkers: People who are walking themselves thin.

Thinwalking: Walking as fast as you comfortably can for as long as you comfortably can.

Thinwalking Story: Exercised muscles pulling fat from storage to "recharge their batteries" and build themselves up.

Thrival Level (of Body Function): Calories used for higher-level activities: problem-solving, rapid or prolonged movement, etc. (see, for contrast: **Survival Level**).

Time-lapse Camera: Device for detecting motion in apparently-immobile objects (plants, usually.)

Tortoise: Slow-moving animal of fable that always wins the race against the faster hare, because of his concentration on the task at hand.

Two-for-One Exchange: What Thinwalking provides: every "unit" you walk gives you two "units" of benefit (see also: **One-for-one Exchange**).

Waistline: Home away from home for all excess calories, where they get temporarily stored as body fat (see also: **"The Man who Came to Dinner"**).

"Wasting Food:" Utterly impossible thing to do (the food is already "wasted" by the time it gets to you), but still considered by many to be the greatest crime a child can commit — especially, for some reason, an overweight child (see also: **"Cleaning your Plate"**).

Water: What your body surrounds salt molecules with, to keep them from killing you; therefore, the first thing the body eliminates when you remove salt from your diet, as you do on every "diet."

Zero: The number of times you should weigh yourself, in the course of a lifetime.

Zombie: The "living dead" (see also: **Starvation Diet**).

FREE!

Thinwalker T-Shirt!

This beautiful, 50/50 T-shirt
can be yours, absolutely free! Just send:

- A PHOTOCOPY ("Xerox") of this page, with the bottom all filled out (pages torn out of books will NOT be accepted);
- A register receipt for *Walk Yourself Thin,* either validated by your retailer or with the book's title printed on it;
- A check or money order for $4.00, to cover the costs of shipping and handling.

Moon River Publishing • P.O. Box 5244 • Ventura, CA 93005

Yes, David:
I'll be PROUD to wear my Free THINWALKER T-shirt. I'd like the following size in a: (check one)
   ❑ Blue Shirt with White Ink
   ❑ White Shirt with Blue Ink
_____Med.   _____Lge.   _____XL   _____XXL   _____XXXL
Send my shirt to: (please print)

Name _____

Address _____

City/State/Zip _____

Phone No. (very important) (_____) _____
In addition, I would like the following shirt(s) sent to:
❑ The above address.   ❑ The address(es) on the enclosed, separate sheet.
Total No. of Additional Shirts of Each Size: _____Med. _____Lge. _____ XL _____XXL _____XXXL
I agree to pay $9.95 for each shirt sent along with my Free one and $13.95 for the first shirt, plus $9.95 for any additional shirts, sent to each different address (please indicate quantities and sizes going to each additional address).

Enclosed please find $4.00 check or money order to cover the costs of shipping and handling my Free shirt, plus $_____ for any additional shirts that I've ordered.

Or please bill my: (check one) _____ Visa _____MasterCard for the full amount due:
Account No._____Exp. Date _____
Account Name (if different from above name)_____
In addition, I would like more copies of *Walk Yourself Thin.* Please send _____ copies to the above address and _____ copies to the addresses indicated on a separate, enclosed sheet (please list number of copies going to each address). I agree to pay $12.95 for each book, plus $4.00 shipping and handling for each separate order (separate address).

The total amount due is enclosed (check or money order), or charge that amount to the above credit card.

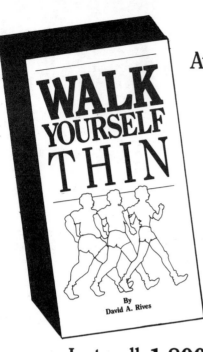

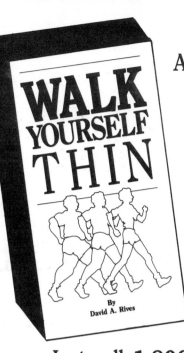

Now
Available!

The entire
WALK YOURSELF THIN
Program
on
AUDIOCASSETTE!!

" ... brilliant!"
" ... what fun!"
" ... perfect complement to the book!"

Just call **1-800-THINWALK** to order.

PHOTOCOPY ("Xerox") this page (pages torn out of books will NOT be ccepted), fill out the coupon below, and send it to Moon River Publishing.

Moon River Publishing • P.O. Box 5244 • Ventura, CA 93005

ar David:

, I'd love to have the audiocassette program. Please send _____ copies to

me _____

dress _____

y/State/Zip _____

one No. (_____) _____

closed please find check or money order (made out to Moon River Publishing) for $29.95 each audiocassette program, plus $3.00 shipping and handling for each order.

bill my (check one): _____ Visa _____ MasterCard

count No._____ Exp. Date_____

count Name (if different from above) _____

o, please send me one Free THINWALKER T-shirt for eacch cassette program ordered. es needed are (indicate number of each):

_____ Med. _____ Lge. _____ XL _____ XXL _____ XXXL _____ XXXXL

dditional shirts available at $9.95 each, plus $3.00 shipping and handling).